The Complete Will Kit

Jens C. Appel, III

F. Bruce Gentry

JOHN WILEY & SONS

New York · Chichester · Brisbane · Toronto · Singapore

This book is dedicated to our parents:

William James Gentry, Sr.
Virginia Reese Gentry

J. C. Appel
Elizabeth Chitwood Appel

Library of Congress Cataloging in Publication Data:

Appel, Jens C., 1948–
   The complete will kit/by Jens C. Appel III and F. Bruce Gentry.
     p. cm.
   Includes bibliographical references.
   ISBN 0-471-51296-6. — ISBN 0-471-51295-8 (pbk.)
    1. Wills—United States—Popular works.   2. Executors and
administrators—United States—Popular works.   3. Estate planning—
United States—Popular works. I. Gentry, F. Bruce, 1946–
II. Title.
KF755.Z9A45   1990
346.7305′2—dc20
[347.30652]   89-29834

Printed in the United States of America

10 9 8 7 6 5 4 3 2 1

Foreword

No legal document has greater importance in today's complex world than a thoughtfully prepared will. Consider the consequences of not having a will. If you die intestate—that is, without leaving a valid will—the state will write your will for you. In the absence of a legal and valid will, your estate will be distributed in accordance with the laws of the state in which you live. The distribution may bear no resemblance to what you wanted. Loved ones may receive little or nothing, while strangers, even the state, may wind up with the lion's share of your hard-earned assets. Perhaps of greater importance, without expressing your wishes through a will, you lose the opportunity to specify who should administer your estate and who should serve as guardian of your minor children. Despite the importance of a will, the surprising fact remains that only one out of three adult Americans enjoys the vital protection of a valid will.

Now, with Bruce Gentry's and Jens Appel's *The Complete Will Kit,* you have at your fingertips everything you need to prepare your first will or revise an existing will. The text provides step-by-step instructions in plain language, free of complicated legal terms and phrases. What makes *The Complete Will Kit* particularly convenient to use are the many illustrations of the types of provisions to consider and how they may be stated appropriately. This valuable, comprehensive book even includes an Executor's guide so that your estate may be handled more efficiently. And, of course, all the actual forms necessary to prepare a professional-looking and valid will or codicil are included.

Recognizing that many people avoid preparing a will because of costly legal fees, we at the Consumer Law Foundation believe *The Complete Will Kit* is the perfect alternative. But, even if you decide to have a lawyer draft your will, or already have such a will, we encourage you to use *The Complete Will Kit*. As you read through the book, you'll have the opportunity to consider many suggestions and alternative ways to plan your estate, techniques that you may otherwise overlook. *The Complete Will Kit* can be a great ally in this most important undertaking—protecting the ones you most care about. I wish you every success as you explore its helpful information and put its valuable contents to work for you today!

ARNOLD S. GOLDSTEIN
President
Consumer Law Foundation

Preface

Throughout your adult lifetime, you have the opportunity to write, revise, amend, and rewrite your will. Later—the time most people set aside to write their wills—is often too late. A will should be prepared early in the adult years, and as your estate plan changes, it should be rewritten or amended. Writing a valid will is a simple process that can be easily repeated whenever necessary. Because your personal, family, and estate situations change over time, your first will is seldom your last.

This book is a guide to the process of writing a will and includes eight complete sets of detachable will forms and related documents. At many times in life, only a brief, simple will is necessary to express your entire estate plan. With one of the forms in this book and adequate preparation, such a will can be completed quickly. The will forms of different lengths offer flexibility as you, your marital status, and your estate plan change over time. Related documents include self-proving certificates, codicils, and letters of instruction. Preparing your will with this book takes little time and effort, particularly when weighed against the consequences of not having one.

At some point in life, many of us are confronted with the task of being the Executor or Administrator of an estate. Chapter 6, a guide to the Executor's duties, is included to help you, as well as your Executor, when that time comes. This step-by-step guide, and the State Summary in Chapter 9, alert you to the requirements and responsibilities involved in settling an estate.

The information in the book is presented in plain, direct language, using few legal terms or phrases. The text is complemented by sample documents that illustrate a variety of estate planning situations based on the experiences of four generations of the fictitious Light family. Chapter 5, which narrates the growth of this family's estate, includes completed samples of each of the blank forms that are provided at the back of the book, and Chapter 8 presents a completed U.S. Estate Tax Return. Property inventory, personal, and Executor record sheets are provided to help you organize estate assets and information, and key information for each state is summarized in a useful guide.

A basic knowledge of wills, estate planning methods, and probate will allow you to make informed choices at any time in life. If you find that your estate requires a detailed plan beyond the scope of this book, do not hestitate to seek additional assistance. Preparing an outline of your estate plan and organizing your personal data using the information and the record sheets in this book will save valuable (and expensive) time if you need to consult an attorney or other professional.

We respect your ability to apply this material to your personal situation and, with care and thought, confidently write your own will. We urge promptness, as you, your family, and others you care for can benefit only from a will that is executed properly and that is available when needed.

F. BRUCE GENTRY
JENS C. APPEL, III

Salem, Virginia
1990

Acknowledgments

We wish to express our appreciation to Naomi Smith and Charles E. Lynn, Jr., for their invaluable assistance in the preparation of the manuscript and the documents. Special thanks are due our wives, Amelia Hough Gentry and Linda Riddle Appel, and our daughters, Amy, Morgen, Joy, and Jade, for their enduring support, understanding, and encouragement during the long preparation of this book. Finally, we wish to thank all those who have helped us to develop a simple approach to estate planning by sharing with us their thoughts, experiences, and concerns over the years.

Contents

C H A P T E R **5**   *A Family and Its Estate: A Story with Sample Documents*   **55**

C H A P T E R **6**   *Executor's Guide*   **77**

C H A P T E R **7**   *Taxes*   **91**

CHAPTER **8** *U.S. Estate Tax Return: Sample Form 706*   **99**

CHAPTER **9** *State Summary*   **127**

Glossary   *141*

Index   *145*

Introduction

The *Complete Will Kit* is a lifetime reference guide to basic estate planning and preparing a will. Recognizing that estate plans change over time, this book provides eight detachable will forms in the Document Set to help you take action, both now and in the future. The text clearly explains the correct procedure for executing a valid will and summarizes key estate planning requirements of all fifty states and the District of Columbia. When your personal situation and estate plan change, you may revoke any previous will or codicil by simply executing a new will. By understanding the simple process of writing, amending, and rewriting a will, you can protect your family and your estate through the years.

Because it is flexible and can be quickly changed, a will is the most responsive document of estate planning. A will can specify guardians for dependents. A will can include gifts of treasured personal property, charitable bequests, and even forgiveness of personal debts and notes. Another advantage offered by a will is the ability to make immediate changes in your plans. Unlike trusts and other estate planning methods that require considerable time and expense to modify, a will can be updated quickly. Even extensive use of trusts rarely eliminates the need for a valid will.

A thorough review of the book can alert you to many options that are available to you when you write a will or make other estate plans. Your will should be current and reflect your plans accurately at all times. Awareness of your options, along with common sense and good judgment, should enable you confidently to protect your estate.

About the Book

The purpose of the *Complete Will Kit* is to provide the reader with a basic knowledge of estate planning and serve as an action guide to the process of writing a will. Simple, direct language is used, and words that may be unfamiliar are explained in the text and defined in the Glossary. Gender-neutral terms are used for those words that have both masculine and feminine forms, such as "Executor/Executrix." Samples are used extensively throughout the text, and common estate planning concerns are illustrated in a series of sample wills based on the experiences of four generations of the fictitious Light family.

The Executor's guide, with its step-by-step explanation of how to settle an estate, removes the mystery from the probate process. Detachable Executor data sheets provide space to list information needed to settle an estate. A series of inventory sheets, keyed to U.S. Estate Tax Return schedules, is included in the Record Set for your convenience. State and federal taxes are discussed, and a completed sample U.S. Estate Tax Return is presented. A working knowledge of the process of settling an estate and estate taxes helps you plan effectively. The remainder of this Introduction is a brief orientation to the components of a simple will.

Sample Will

A will is simply a document, signed before two (or more) witnesses, that records your intent for the distribution of your estate. Such a will is known as a testamentary will and is recognized in all 50 states and the District of Columbia. The people involved with a testamentary will are as follows.

Testator. A person who writes a valid will is called a Testator. A will identifies the Testator by his or her full name and legal address. The Testator executes a will by signing and dating the document in front of witnesses.

Executor. Your will names an Executor for your estate and empowers him or her to act for you. This person will be responsible for administering the estate and carrying out the provisions of your will.

Beneficiary. The person or organization you name to receive all, or a portion, of your estate is known as a beneficiary. For clarity, each beneficiary should be identified by full name and relationship.

Witnesses. Witnesses are persons who together see the Testator sign and date a will and who then sign the will at the Testator's request. Witnesses should be persons who are not related to the Testator and who are not mentioned in the will. Witnesses must be adults and should list their addresses when signing.

In the following sample will, a 58-year-old man leaves his entire estate to his wife, except for three specific bequests to his son, daughter, and church. He has also included a provision specifying that if his wife does not survive him, his estate is to be divided equally between his children. The will was executed in 1930, with two of his neighbors as witnesses. Basic components of this sample will are keyed alphabetically to brief explanations. (See Figures 1 and 2.)

LAST WILL AND TESTAMENT

(A) I, _____ Paul Samuel Light _____ , resident

of the __County__ of ____Botetourt____ in the State of ___VIRGINIA___ ,

(B) being of sound mind, do make and declare the following to be my LAST WILL AND TESTAMENT and expressly revoke all my prior wills and codicils and certify that I am not acting under undue influence, duress or menace.

I. EXECUTOR

(C) I appoint _____ Naomi Lee Spencer Light, my wife, ____ EXECUTOR of this my LAST WILL AND TESTAMENT. If this EXECUTOR is unable to serve for any reason,

(D) then I appoint _____ Carroll Abraham Light, my son, _____ EXECUTOR.

(E) The EXECUTOR is empowered to carry out all provisions of this WILL.
The EXECUTOR shall have all statutory powers available under State law.

(F) The EXECUTOR named shall not be required to post surety bond. I direct that no outside appraisal be made of my estate, unless required for estate tax purposes.

II. BEQUESTS

(G) I give my entire estate to my beloved wife, Naomi Lee Spencer Light, with the exception of the following three bequests.

(H) 1. To my son, Carroll Abraham Light, I give my Parker 12 gauge shotgun.

(H) 2. To my daughter, Mary Alice Light, I give the sum of two hundred dollars ($200.00).

(I) 3. To my church, Brandy Run Church of God, I give the sum of fifty dollars ($50.00).

(J) If my wife, Naomi Lee Spencer Light, should die before me, then all of my estate, except for the above bequests, I give to my son, Carroll Abraham Light and my daughter, Mary Alice Light, in equal shares.

(K) This concludes my entire Last Will and Testament.

Figure 1

Last Will and Testament

(A) A will sets out the full legal name of the Testator and identifies the jurisdiction of legal residence (city or county and state).

(B) A statement that the Testator is of sound mind and free of outside influence. All previous wills and codicils are declared to be void.

I. EXECUTOR

(C) An Executor, identified by full legal name and relationship, is named to settle the estate.

(D) An alternate Executor is named, again identified by full legal name and relationship.

(E) Powers are granted to the Executor to carry out provisions of the will.

(F) To save expenses to the estate, the Testator directs that no surety bond be required of the Executor and that no outside appraisals of the estate be made.

II. BEQUESTS

(G) The entire estate is left to the primary beneficiary, identified by full legal name and relationship, except for three specific bequests.

(H) Personal property bequests are specific, and beneficiaries are identified by full legal name and relationship.

(I) A specific charitable bequest clearly identifies the organization that is to receive it.

(J) A provision is included specifying how to dispose of the estate if the primary beneficiary dies first.

(K) To safeguard against additions, a statement indicates the end of the entire will.

III. WITNESSED

(L) The Testator must date and sign the will in the presence of all the witnesses together.

(M) The will is identified by the name of the Testator and the date.

(N) Witnesses sign the will using full legal names and listing their addresses. Witnesses should be adults not mentioned in the will.

(L)   IN WITNESS WHEREOF, I have hereunto set my hand this *twenty-ninth* day
       of *October* , 19 *30* .

                                    Paul Samuel Light
                                         (Testator signature)

III. WITNESSED

(M)   This LAST WILL AND TESTAMENT of *Paul Samuel Light*
       was signed and declared to be his/~~her~~ LAST WILL AND TESTAMENT in our presence at his/~~her~~ request
       and in his/~~her~~ presence and the presence of each other as witnesses this *twenty-ninth*

       day of *October* , 19 *30* .

(N)   *James Robert Smuya*   *Rt. 1, Box 293, Springwood, VA.*
       (Witness signature)   *(Address)*

(N)   *Ellen Susan Sawyer - Rt. 1, Box 293, Springwood, VA*
       (Witness signature)   *(Address)*

       _____   _____
       (Witness signature)   *(Address)*

                                    Figure 2

As the preceding sample shows, even a brief will can be complete and effective. To be legally valid, a testamentary will must be properly witnessed. This simple procedure is outlined as follows:

Correct Witness Procedure

1. Have your witnesses together when you are ready to sign your will.
2. Sign and date your will in front of both (or all three) witnesses. (You may cover the contents for privacy, if desired.)
3. Have each witness, in the presence of you and of one another, sign the will and list his or her address.

Your witnesses should be "disinterested," that is, people who are not mentioned in the will and who are not related to you. When you sign (execute) your will, you must do so in front of all your witnesses together. Two adult witnesses are required everywhere in the United States except Louisiana and Vermont, where three witnesses are required. The witnesses verify that you signed your will in their presence and were of sound mind and not acting under the influence of others.

Additional information about estate planning, trusts, and financial planning is available at your local library and bookstores. The local probate court, law libraries, and state taxation departments can all be of assistance and are good sources of current, specific information.

If you decide that you need further professional assistance in preparing your will, be sure to fill out the inventory and data forms and prepare a draft copy of your will. Having your plans outlined and complete estate information available can save time, expense, and error. Most important, such advance planning can ensure that your will expresses an informed and clearly thought out distribution of your property that omits nothing and leaves nothing to chance.

CHAPTER 1

Preparing Your Estate Plan

The Role of Your Will

Estate planning involves the creation, conservation, and eventual distribution of your real and personal property. Although many options and methods are available for the transfer of property, a valid last will remains a cornerstone of effective estate planning. Many estate planning techniques are in common use that allow property to pass outside the probate system. Joint titling of both real and personal assets, gifts, trusts, and other methods of distribution that avoid probate and taxes are common estate planning measures. The role of your will in estate planning is flexible, addressing your personal needs at various stages of your life and setting out your plan for the assets and property not disposed of by other means. Naming an Executor for your estate, specifying guardians for children, or making a gift of a personal treasure to a close friend are typical choices expressed in a will. No matter how extensively you've arranged your estate plan, never neglect the need for a valid will.

As shown by the sample in the Introduction, your will can be a very simple document, setting out your complete plan regarding distribution of your estate. Your will should always reflect your current goals, family needs, and personal decisions. Your will can be amended or revoked and replaced by a new one at any time.

Estate Concerns

You can reasonably expect to write several wills in a lifetime. The process of writing, executing, and maintaining a will should become a routine part of your overall estate plan. Updating your will as needed can help keep it simple, effective, and responsive to your current needs.

The passage of time can make significant changes in your personal, family, and estate situation. The legal responsibilities of property ownership and personal liability begin with adulthood and continue throughout your lifetime. The process of estate planning often begins early with the purchase of life insurance and the execution of a simple will. Your first will, often simple in content, may be supplemented, or supplanted, to take into account guardians, additional beneficiaries, charitable bequests, or other elements of your estate plan. Consider your estate, beneficiaries, and family needs, and plan accordingly when deciding on the content of your will. Bequests and provisions in your will may be as brief or extensive as needed to express your wishes and plans. A simple will is not necessarily short.

Assessing your personal situation is a task you are best qualified to perform. Typical concerns include your health, marital situation, and dependents; the status of your beneficiaries; and the risks involved in your daily life. Your age and health, and that of your beneficiaries, is extremely important in shaping your estate plan. At the early stages of adult life, your assets and responsibilities may be few, requiring only a simple will to transfer your estate to your beneficiaries. At such times, your primary concern may be to assure that your personal property is disposed of in the manner you decide. Automobiles, household goods, jewelry, and electronic, photographic, hobby, or sports equipment may be disposed of in a valid will with little extended planning required. In later years, after a lifetime of changes, the same concerns often apply. The estate planning cycle often begins, and ends, with a simple will.

Changes in your estate plan usually follow important events in your life, including:

- Moving
- Marriage
- Birth or adoption of children
- Divorce
- Remarriage
- Death of grandparents and others of their generation

- Maturity of children
- Birth of grandchildren
- Death of parents and others of their generation
- Growth of estate, including inheritance(s)
- Need for estate tax planning
- Continuing health care needs
- Death of spouse
- Death of beneficiaries

These events can affect the nature of your estate and influence your choice of beneficiaries. Be sure to review your estate plan periodically and address important events that change your estate planning goals and methods.

Special Situations

Basic provisions in your will can adequately address many of the special situations listed in the preceding section. Other estate planning methods, especially trusts, may also be considered in certain situations. As changes occur, your will, along with the other components of your estate plan, should be kept current.

MARRIAGE

Marriage can affect your personal goals, the ownership of property, and your estate plan. Your will, and your spouse's, should address your shared and individual goals. The need for a will is especially critical if you intend your spouse to inherit the majority of your estate. In most states, if there is no will to direct otherwise, your spouse may inherit only a portion of your assets. Also, be aware that all states allow a spouse the right of "elective share." This simply means that your spouse may elect to take the portion of the estate left in your will or an amount defined by state law. Because of the elective share laws, it is virtually impossible to disinherit your legal spouse totally. At all times in married life, each spouse should have a will to express current estate planning goals.

Marriage, of course, has a significant effect on property ownership. In community-property states, each spouse has a one-half interest in all property of the marriage. The property interest of each spouse is individual and, if no other plans are made, should be disposed of in the will. Property owned individually before the marriage remains separate and may also be distributed in a will. If you live in a community-property state, be sure your will specifies how you intend to dispose of the individual property that is a part of your estate. You and your spouse should coordinate your estate plans, and each of you should prepare wills accordingly.

Joint ownership, with right of survivorship, is a common estate planning technique used by married couples, as well as by others who own property together. Property held in joint ownership transfers title to the survivor upon the death of one of the owners. This type of transfer is automatic and avoids probate of the property. Real estate, bank accounts, and other property are often jointly titled by couples as an estate planning measure. Be sure to review deeds, titles, and account agreements that are titled jointly to ensure that "right of survivorship" is included. Joint owners may plan for the remote possibility of simultaneous death by naming an alternate beneficiary in their wills. If both partners die together and their wills agree on an alternate beneficiary, that person will receive the property once held jointly by both. For this reason, it is extremely important that spouses' wills agree on major provisions, especially the choice of alternate beneficiaries and Executor. In some states, a form of real property ownership, "tenants by the entirety," is available to married couples only. This type of ownership also transfers title automatically to the remaining spouse.

Trusts and life estates are options that can offer many advantages and may be considered as part of your estate plan. Trusts are often used to provide income to a surviving spouse or other beneficiaries while the assets of the trust are conserved for future distribution. There are several types of trusts and methods of establishing them to achieve different purposes. You and your spouse should discuss your goals, tax position, and anticipated income needs when considering trusts. A life estate can guarantee your spouse or other beneficiary the right to occupy real property, such as a house or farm, while allowing the title to be transferred to another beneficiary. Title transfers prior to death avoid probate and, because a life estate is a liability against real property, may lower the value of the taxable estate.

Divorce and remarriage can be of special concern to those preparing an estate plan. If you or your spouse have been married previously, be sure to check for accuracy all titles, deeds, and insurance policies acquired during the previous marriage. If either spouse has children by a previous marriage, choices must be made regarding their place, if any, in your estate plan. For those who are married, agreement and coordination are essential to effective estate planning.

Relationships other than marriage may also affect your estate planning decisions. In some states, those who live together continuously for a period of time may be considered legally married, even though no formal marriage ceremony has taken place. Common-law marriages of this type may have significant impact on the way an estate is divided. If you or one of your beneficiaries maintains a living relationship with someone who is not a legal spouse, you should consider the implications carefully. States that currently recognize common-law marriage are Alabama, Colorado, Georgia, Idaho, Iowa, Kansas, Montana, Ohio, Oklahoma, Pennsylvania, Rhode Island, South Carolina, and Texas. The District of Columbia also recognizes common-law marriages.

In summary, those who are currently married, considering marriage, or maintaining a relationship that could have the legal status of marriage should take special care when preparing an estate plan. Each spouse should have a will, and the major provisions should not conflict or disagree. Spouses who have named each other as sole or primary beneficiary should always name alternates to receive the estate if both die simultaneously.

CHILDREN AND DEPENDENTS

If you are responsible for the care of minor children, you should nominate a guardian for them in your will. While your wishes are not strictly binding, the probate court usually appoints your nominee as guardian when you express your intent in your will. Designating a person to serve as guardian of minor children in the case of the simultaneous death of both parents is important, and the wills of both parents should agree regarding the designation of the contingent guardian. Close family members, including the spouse and extended family, are usually relied on to provide care for minor children until they reach maturity. A healthy surviving spouse, provided adequate financial resources through insurance or estate assets, is usually the best choice for dependent care. If you are single or lack family resources, the importance of this type of planning becomes more critical.

Plans for dependents, especially those regarding care, education, religious affiliation, and management of assets, should be outlined and discussed with your chosen guardian. The guardians you appoint must consent and be acceptable to the court. Financial support, especially over a long period of time, may require a trust or other arrangements.

● **Example**

If my wife, Jo Anne Stone Light, does not survive me by more than 180 days, then I give my entire estate to my daughter, Linda Lee Light, and my son, Paul Abraham Light, in equal shares, and I appoint Abraham Lee Light, my father, as guardian of my children until they attain their majority.

CHILDREN: UNEQUAL SHARES

If you have no will, your children—minor and adult, biological and adopted, legitimate and illegitimate—may have an equal claim on your estate. Most states also provide your unborn (pretermitted) children a share of your estate if you die intestate. Often, parents have children with unequal needs or have concerns about the ability of a particular child to manage assets. In later stages of estate planning, prior gifts made to children may affect the terms of your will. Providing for children requires special care as you outline your estate plan. When children are minors or require continuing care, you may consider estate planning methods beyond your will that provide income and financial security over time. If you have minor or adult children that you intend to exclude from your estate or treat differently in your will, take special care to spell out your intentions.

Your will may include special instructions regarding property left to minors. You may specify a person to hold and care for gifts of property to those who are immature or, by law, unable to take possession.

● **Example**

I direct my son, Frederick Roger Hale, who is my appointed Executor, to keep the Browning shotgun, SN 67890, that I have given to my grandson, Charles James Hale, until he has reached maturity and is able to safely assume possession, or reaches the age of 18 years.

If you plan to exclude a particular child from your estate, be sure to state that intention in your will. If you fail to mention one child while leaving gifts to others, the court may rule that you simply overlooked that child and may award him or her a share proportionate to those of your other children. Be sure provisions regarding children are clear, complete, and direct.

● **Example**

I have purposely made no provision for my son, William Samuel Stull, because I have neither seen him nor heard from him in the last thirty years.

Be sure to list the reasons for unequal treatment of your children in your will. Unequal division of your estate can often result from prior gifts or loans made to your children.

● **Example**

I give my entire estate to my son, James Carl Stull. I have intentionally made no provision for my other son, Howard Charles Stull, since I previously purchased an eighty-acre farm in Pasco County, Florida, for him in accordance with his expressed wishes.

Making unequal provisions in your will should always be planned carefully. Children who are treated unequally, or who are excluded from your will, are a likely source of will contests.

DISINHERITANCE

Disinheritance usually applies to immediate family members (an only child, for example) who would have a claim on your estate if you had no will or if your will were declared invalid. Note that Louisiana is the only state in which you cannot disinherit your children. If you disinherit an immediate family member, it is always wise to state your reasons for doing so in your will. In most cases, you may effectively disinherit anyone other than your named beneficiaries by simply not including them in your will. If you wish, you may also include a statement in your will specifically omitting all others.

● **Example**

I hereby specifically exclude from my estate any and all other persons not named previously in this, my Last Will and Testament.

CAUTION: Completely disinheriting your legal spouse is virtually impossible. In any case, your spouse will be able to take an elective "forced" share of the estate. Remember, disinheriting a close family member can cause controversy in your family. Family members who feel that they have been unfairly disinherited are the source of most will challenges. If you have reason to believe that someone will contest your will, recognize that he or she will probably engage an attorney, and take special care when preparing your will. A properly executed (signed and witnessed) will is very difficult to challenge successfully.

Many of the special situations encountered at different stages of estate planning may be addressed with simple provisions in your will. Evaluating your personal situation and your goals is necessary to determine if additional estate planning measures are needed. If continuing care of dependents, conservation of assets for future generations, or estate taxes are a concern, you should consider a trust or other arrangement. Health and medical expenses are also concerns that can affect estate planning decisions. Two common estate planning techniques that address continuing care, conservation of assets, and health concerns are the living will and the power of attorney. Another is the trust, which is treated is some detail in the next section.

LIVING WILL

For reasons that include the recognition that large medical bills can rapidly erode an estate, some people choose to record their wishes regarding extended life-support measures. A living will is a signed, dated, and properly witnessed document in which you state *in advance* your wishes regarding the use of life-support procedures in cases of terminal illness, serious incapacitation, or prolonged coma. Most states currently recognize living wills (refer to the State Summary in Chapter 9); however, witness procedures and notarizing requirements vary. It is especially important to notarize living wills in those states that have no legislation relating to them. You may obtain current information about living wills in your state by contacting your doctor or the Concern for Dying Foundation, 250 West 57th Street, New York, NY 10107.

POWER OF ATTORNEY

A durable power of attorney is another document that may be of value in the later stages of estate planning. A power of attorney is a signed, witnessed, and notarized statement appointing someone as "your attorney in fact," with specified powers to act on your behalf. A durable power of attorney continues in effect in the event of the later disability or incompetence of the maker. You must be able to have complete trust in the person who holds a durable power of attorney, as he or she is legally authorized to act on your behalf. For this reason, consider this step carefully and only when needed.

Trusts

A trust is simply defined as giving assets or property to one party (a trustee) to hold, use, or manage for another party (the trust beneficiary). A trust is legally established by the witnessed and notarized execution of a declaration of trust by the creator of the trust (also called the settlor, grantor, trustor, or donor). The trust agreement empowers the trustee to administer the trust and sets out its terms and conditions.

Many techniques of estate planning can be set up with little or no outside help. For example, tax-deductible gifts of up to $10,000 each may be made to children and grandchildren each year by each parent. The preparation of a will; joint titling of real estate and accounts, with a specified right of survivorship; and payment of life insurance policy proceeds to a named beneficiary can all be arranged easily, without ongoing outside assistance required. A trust, however, requires the services of a trustee, who is empowered to oversee the operation of the trust, in accordance with the guidance contained in the basic trust agreement. Since a trust cannot be effectively used for estate planning purposes without outside assistance, the following material is intended to provide a general overview of trusts so that the type of trust needed can be identified. After review of this material, it is suggested that the components of the trust desired be listed in outline form to provide an informed basis for proceeding with outside assistance. The Trust Checklist is provided for this purpose. (See pages 20 and 21.)

PURPOSES OF TRUSTS

Reasons for establishing a trust include:

- Providing for continuing care and education of minor children (or grandchildren)
- Providing income for a surviving spouse
- Providing for continuing care of a dependent or incompetent adult
- Providing the assistance and the security of professional management of assets
- Minimizing federal estate taxes if the combined estate (of husband and wife) will exceed $600,000 upon the death of the surviving spouse
- Minimizing state inheritance taxes
- Avoiding the expense, delay, and public record involved in the probate process

THE TRUST ENTITY

The establishment of a trust creates a separate legal entity, the trust, which has ownership and/or title of property transferred to it. As a separate legal entity, the trust must be given a Federal Employer Identification Number (FEIN), and separate state and federal income tax returns must be filed if the trust's income exceeds $600 annually. Generally, the trust holds title to all its assets, is managed by a trustee, and is owned by the beneficiary(ies). Functionally, a trust is very similar to a private investment corporation. The trustee should keep accurate accounts and report on the trust's status to the beneficiaries (owners) on a regular basis.

THE TIMING OF TRUST DISTRIBUTION

The reasons for establishing a trust affect its terms. An arrangement suitable for one stage of family life, addressing care of minor children in the event of the death of one or both parents, becomes functionally obsolete when the children reach adulthood and are presumed capable of managing their own affairs. A trust to pass on family real estate to the next generation may be established whenever circumstances warrant it. Establishing a trust to provide a source of funds for the continuing care of a spouse or relative who has, or may have, medical problems is often a concern in later life. Tax planning reasons for establishing a trust are directly related to the present and anticipated value of your estate.

A trust can be structured to pay all, or a portion of, the trust principal to the trust beneficiary(ies) at various times, either on specific dates, such as birthdays, or over multiyear periods.

Examples of timing trust principal distribution include:

- All to beneficiary(ies) on January 1, 2000.
- Each beneficiary's principal to be paid in full upon his or her twenty-fifth birthday.
- Beneficiary to receive one-third of the principal 10 years from the date of the trust agreement, one-half of the remaining principal 5 years later, and the balance of the principal 20 years from the date of the trust agreement.

10 years	⅓
15 years (⅔ ÷ ½)	⅓
20 years (Balance)	⅓

- All to beneficiaries upon sale of trust assets, per trust agreement.

When the principal balance of the trust is fully paid to the trust beneficiary(ies), the trust is terminated.

Trusts can be established either on a revocable or an irrevocable basis. An irrevocable trust cannot be changed, whereas a revocable trust can be terminated at the trustee's discretion. At present, there are no federal income or estate tax advantages to a revocable trust.

THE TRUSTEE

Clearly, the person or organization chosen as trustee has a significant bearing on how the trust is structured. If a third-party trustee, either an individual or an organization, is appointed, the trustee should be bonded in the amount of the trust to protect the interests of the beneficiary(ies). Compensation of the trustee for investment, management, disbursement, and state and federal tax filings should be established and agreed on before a trust is set up. Third-party trustee fees vary with the size, term, and complexity of the trust, and it is wise to obtain several quotes. If the trust has a relatively long term, it is also desirable to select an alternate trustee to serve in case the first trustee becomes incapacitated or is otherwise unable to serve.

Trusts can be organized either as "living" trusts (*inter vivos* trusts) or as "testamentary" trusts (established upon death). If you set up a living trust, you can also be the trustee. Generally, a revocable trust is preferable, if you plan to act as the trustee or wish to assess the performance of a third-party trustee.

THE FUNDING OF TRUSTS

Living trusts are funded with wholly owned assets such as cash, stocks, bonds, and real estate. A testamentary trust can be funded with wholly owned assets or life insurance policy proceeds. The initial funding of a trust is its principal. Funds earned from the trust principal, such as interest, dividends, and rents, are considered as trust income. Many trusts are designed to preserve the principal until termination, with the trust income being distributed to the trust beneficiaries in a timely manner for their benefit. In other cases, the trust may be structured to reinvest all income, thereby creating a larger principal balance to be paid out when the trust is terminated.

If the trust is funded with real estate, you may also grant a lifetime-use provision for a spouse or others, particularly if they are not to be beneficiaries of the trust upon its termination. This is accomplished by adding a life estate interest clause to the deed of the property involved before its transfer to the trust. A beneficiary of a trust has vested ownership in all, or part of, the trust principal and income. Unless otherwise specified, ownership of a trust interest is an asset to the owner and, as such, can become a part of the owner's estate.

Trust Checklist

PURPOSE(S) OF TRUST

_____   Continuing care/income

_____   Maintenance of ownership

_____   Timed distribution of assets

_____   Privacy/avoiding probate

_____   Tax considerations

TYPE OF TRUST

_____   Testamentary trust

_____   Living trust *(inter vivos)*

NATURE OF TRUST

_____   Irrevocable

_____   Revocable

TRUSTEE

_____   Third party

_____   Self/owner(s)

TRUST ASSET(S)

_____   Real estate

_____   Stocks/bonds

_____   Cash

_____   Income-producing asset(s)

SOURCE OF TRUST ASSETS

_____   Lifetime transfer(s)

_____   Estate

_____   Life insurance proceeds

TERM OF TRUST

_____   Years

TRUST OWNERS/INCOME BENEFICIARY(IES)

_____

_____

_____

_____

TIMING OF TRUST DISTRIBUTION

Income _____

_____

_____

Principal/Asset(s) _____

_____

_____

Date _____

CHAPTER 2

Writing Your Will

Will: (a) A legal statement of a person's wishes concerning the disposal of his property after death; (b) the document containing this.

Webster's New Twentieth Century Dictionary, 2nd Ed.,
Simon & Schuster, New York, 1983

Any capable adult, by following simple formalities, can prepare and execute a valid will with little difficulty. Because, in most states, the laws regarding wills have their origins in English Common Law, the form and formalities of a testamentary will are clearly established. Although there is no strictly "standard" format, the will forms in this book, as do most wills, contain an opening clause, provisions to name and empower an Executor, a space for bequests, and an attestation clause for signing by witnesses. This chapter discusses the basic form of a testamentary will and key information regarding your Executor and witnesses. Other forms related to your will, self-proving certificates, and codicils, are also explained.

Forms and Formalities

Regardless of the content, complexity, and length of your will, it shares common characteristics with all other wills. A testamentary will must contain a statement of intent, be signed by the Testator, and be witnessed by at least two persons (three in Louisiana and Vermont) who are not connected to your estate. The will forms in this book contain an opening clause to identify the Testator and declare intent and an "attestation" clause for signing by witnesses. The forms also contain a section to name and empower your chosen

Executor and, of course, a section reserved for bequests. Most testamentary wills are similar in form, no matter how they are prepared.

The opening clause is included in all testamentary (witnessed) wills to identify the Testator fully, set out the legal jurisdiction of residence, and declare that the document is the last will and testament, revoking all prior wills and codicils. Though not required, most opening clauses include a statement asserting the soundness of mind and memory of the Testator and stating that the will has been prepared free of influence or threat by others.

● Example ───────────────────────────────

Last Will and Testament

I, ____Naomi Lee Spencer Light____, resident of the ____County____ of ____Botetourt____ in the State of ____Virginia____, being of sound mind, do make and declare the following to be my LAST WILL AND TESTAMENT and expressly revoke all my prior wills and codicils and certify that I am not acting under undue influence, duress, or menace.

───────────────────────────────●

Your Executor

The "Executor" section on the will forms provides space to list your chosen Executor and an alternate. Your Executor, usually a beneficiary, will handle the details of settling your estate and fulfill the terms of your will. Naming an alternate Executor can ensure that a person you have chosen administers your estate if your first-named Executor is unable or unwilling to serve.

● Example ───────────────────────────────

I. EXECUTOR

I appoint ____Paul Samuel Light, my husband____, EXECUTOR of this my LAST WILL AND TESTAMENT. If this EXECUTOR is unable to serve for any reason, then I appoint ____Carroll Abraham Light, my son____, EXECUTOR.

───────────────────────────────●

You may name, with only a few limitations, any person you choose as the Executor of your estate. In all states, the person chosen must be competent, of legal age, and a U.S. citizen. It is usually practical to have an Executor who lives in the same state; however, it is not a requirement. To save expense and maintain privacy, most people name as their Executor their spouse, a major beneficiary, a family member, or a friend. When complicated or extensive estate administration is required, your choice of Executor becomes more critical. Trust and confidence, as well as cost, are important considerations when you choose your Executor.

Be sure to discuss and confirm your plans with your chosen Executor. A person nominated as Executor can refuse appointment or petition the court to be released from his or her duties after appointment if unable to serve. In such cases, the alternate Executor named in your will is appointed.

The Role of the Executor

The Executor of an estate is required to:

- Submit the will to the court for probate to establish its validity.
- Inventory all assets of the estate.
- Collect funds due the testator.
- Pay just debts of the testator.
- File state and federal tax returns.
- Distribute the estate in accordance with the terms of the will.
- Submit receipts from all beneficiaries and a final accounting of receipts and disbursements to the court.

The Executor will act as your agent to collect and conserve the assets of your estate and pay expenses, debts, and taxes on your behalf. After all liabilities are paid, the Executor distributes the remainder of the estate according to the terms of the will. Any capable, competent adult should have little difficulty in settling a simple estate. After the estate is closed by the court, the duties and powers of the Executor are ended.

You may name Co-Executors to share the duties of administering your estate. Naming a Co-Executor who is unlikely to predecease you or to move away from your community guards against problems created by distance and unpredictability. Frequently, adult children are named as Co-Executors, particularly if the estate is to be divided between them. If extensive or complicated estate administration is needed, you may consider naming a bank, a financial institution, an attorney, or another qualified person as Executor. Bear in mind that your Executor can employ professional assistance and therefore need not perform all the duties of closing the estate alone.

If you've appointed a major beneficiary as Executor, there is usually no reason to compensate that person for performing the duties required to settle your estate. Executor fees are a liability to the estate and therefore reduce the amount available to the beneficiaries. If your Executor feels that the specified compensation is inadequate, he or she may petition the court to award reasonable compensation. "Reasonable" compensation is defined in most states as a percentage (usually 3 to 5 percent) of the value of the estate. Avoiding the expense of court-ordered Executor fees is a good reason to name your major beneficiary as Executor. If you are considering someone other than a beneficiary as Executor, discuss your plans carefully, and agree to compensation before making your final selection. Remember, provisions or instructions in a will that keep the estate open for an extended period of time require continuing administration by the Executor.

In order to settle your estate efficiently, your Executor will need certain information about you, your beneficiaries, and the real and personal property you own. The simplest method of providing that information is to discuss your plans fully with your Executor and furnish him or her with the needed information. Your Executor plays a vital role in your estate plan and should be as informed as necessary to act on your behalf. The Record Set in this book includes Executor Data Sheets, which list the basic information your Executor will need.

The Executor of your estate is required by law to pay your debts, funeral expenses, and taxes. Because of the legal requirement that these obligations be met, there is no need to specify their payment in your will. All states grant sufficient powers to allow your Executor to settle your estate.

● Example

The EXECUTOR is empowered to carry out all provisions of this WILL.

The EXECUTOR shall have all statutory powers available under State law.

In addition to the nomination of the Executor and alternate, and the designation of duties and powers, a clause is frequently included in wills to free the Executor from obtaining a surety bond. A surety bond, equal to the value of the estate, is usually required by law if direction is not included specifically to release the Executor from obtaining a bond. When the Executor you nominate is a person you know and trust, the cost of such a bond is an unnecessary expense to your estate. The first six will forms in this book contain this printed clause.

● Example

The EXECUTOR named shall not be required to post surety bond.

Those who wish to guard against the possibility of illegal or irresponsible administration by the Executor may specify that the Executor post a surety bond. Some situations, although few, may call for this measure. The last set of will forms does not include a printed statement to release the Executor from bond requirements, although you may write or type one in. If you wish to require a bond of your Executor, you should make a statement to that effect.

● **Example** ————————————————————————————————————

I direct that the named Executor post a surety bond equal to the value of my estate.

——●

NAMING AN OUT-OF-STATE EXECUTOR

All states allow nonresidents to act as Executors, and most states place no restrictions or additional requirements on nonresidents. States with restrictions usually require a nonresident Executor to be a primary beneficiary or close family member. In some states, a nonresident Executor is required to secure a bond or have a state resident act as a personal representative. Those who name a nonresident Executor should have important estate and personal information available to the Executor and discuss any special plans or instructions with him or her. Your Executor will need detailed personal and financial information in order to settle your estate as quickly and inexpensively as possible. Remember, naming someone in a distant state as your Executor will involve additional travel and expense. Whenever possible, it is best to name a resident of your state as your Executor.

Outside Appraisal of the Estate

An additional clause included in many wills directs that no outside appraisal of the estate be made. An outside appraisal is usually unnecessary unless the estate is substantial, complex, or ordered by the court for estate tax valuation. In most states, one or more appraisals may be required, with the costs being paid from the estate, unless a specific direction such as the following is included.

● **Example** ————————————————————————————————————

I direct that no outside appraisal of my estate be made unless required for estate tax purposes.

——●

Bequests

Because the primary purpose of a will is to dispose of the estate of the Testator, all wills contain bequests. The bequests you make in your will generally fall into two categories: specific bequests and a residuary bequest. Specific bequests are gifts of specifically identified assets or stated amounts of money.

● **Example**

I give my 1936 Ford Sedan, SN 12345765, to my brother, Samuel Gordon Stull.

A residual bequest disposes of all the property not set out in specific bequests. A residuary bequest in a will disposes of personal items and other property not specifically included in other bequests.

● **Example**

I give all the residue of my estate to the American Heart Association, 706 Fifth Avenue, New York, New York, for the general purposes of the organization.

Witnessing Your Will

A testamentary will must be witnessed according to the statutory requirements of the state in which it is written. The role of witnesses is simple but extremely important. The witnesses attest that you signed and dated your will in their presence and were of sound mind and acting voluntarily when you did so. The witnesses attest to these facts by signing and dating your will as witnesses. If anyone questions the authenticity of your will, the witnesses may be called upon to verify that you signed the document in their presence. For this reason, the witnesses should always list their full names and addresses. The basic procedure to follow when you are ready to sign and date your will is as follows.

1. Choose your witnesses carefully, and be sure to have them available when you are ready to sign and date your will.
2. Sign and date your will in the presence of all your witnesses. (You may orally declare to the witnesses that the document is your last will and testament.)

3. Have each witness sign and date the document in your presence and in the presence of each other. Be sure witnesses list their residential addresses.

Following this simple procedure can help assure that your will is declared valid and quickly admitted for probate. Choosing your witnesses carefully is also an important consideration when preparing your will.

Two witnesses are required in all states except Louisiana and Vermont, which require three. You may have more than the required number of witnesses but never less. Your witnesses must be of legal age, of sound mind, and, in most states, "disinterested." A disinterested witness is a person who has no interest in your estate, either personally or through others. In many states, witnesses and their immediate families are prohibited by law from sharing in the estate of the Testator, whereas others limit the share of an estate the witnesses may take. In some states, persons who have an interest in your estate are disqualified as witnesses, which can result in your will being declared void. Consider your witnesses carefully; co-workers, friends, neighbors, and fellow church members are often good choices. Choosing witnesses who are stable community members, who are in good health, and who have no interest in your estate is always wise.

Your witnesses must be *together* to see you sign and date your will or codicil. Since your witnesses attest that you are not under duress, menace, or undue influence, you may wish to state that, as well as declaring that the document you are signing is your last will and testament (or codicil). The contents may be kept private; there is no need for your witnesses to have any knowledge of the terms or provisions of the document.

Self-Proving Your Will

When a will is presented to the court, the witnesses may be called to "prove" (verify) their signatures on the document. Most often, a copy of the will or attestation portion is sent to the witnesses, along with an affidavit to sign and return to the court. If your will is contested or questioned by the court, the witnesses will be required to appear or sign an affidavit.

In all but five states (Mississippi, Vermont, Washington, West Virginia, and Wisconsin), self-proving certificates are recognized. A self-proving certificate verifies that the signatures appearing on the will are those of the Testator and witnesses. After being signed by all, the certificate is notarized and attached to the will. A properly completed and notarized self-proving certificate frees your witnesses from appearing when your will is presented to the court. Although there is no requirement that your will be self-proved, it is a step that should be considered. Settling your estate may be delayed if your witnesses move to an unknown address or for some other reason are difficult to locate when needed. To self-prove your will, you and your witnesses must personally appear before a notary public. The notary can complete the self-proving certificate and notarize the document after everyone has signed.

Reviewing Your Will

The purpose of a will is to document clearly the Testator's intent regarding the disposition of the property that constitutes his or her estate. Periodically, review your estate and family situation to ensure that your will meets your needs. When changing personal circumstances make your existing will invalid or obsolete, revising your will is necessary. Whether you are starting with a simple holographic (wholly handwritten) will or a detailed document including many bequests and multiple contingencies, the first step is to note the type of changes that are necessary.

Will Revision Checklist

_____   Legal residence of testator

_____   Designated Executor and alternate

_____   Executor bond requirements

_____   Direction regarding outside appraisals of estate

_____   Executor compensation

_____   Addition or deletion of beneficiaries

_____   Addition or deletion of bequests

_____   Addition or deletion of charitable bequests

_____   Addition or deletion of designated guardian(s)

_____   Legal adulthood of children and grandchildren

_____   Creation or deletion of a trust

_____   Estate tax considerations

_____   Other personal changes

If only simple changes are needed, your current valid will can be amended by the addition of a codicil. If more extensive modification is required, you should simply rewrite your will. In either case, the "testamentary" method, a will or codicil that is signed and dated before witnesses, is recommended.

Codicils

A codicil is simply a document that specifies a change in your current will, and it must reference your current will. A codicil must be executed, signed and dated before witnesses, in the same manner as a will, and should be physically attached to the will it amends. A codicil may be self-proved, in which case it also self-proves the will amended by the codicil.

A codicil can be used to address immediate changes in your estate plans while you formulate a more comprehensive approach. When preparing a codicil, be sure to use full legal names, state relationships, and use specific language to ensure that your intent is clear. A codicil references your current will by your full legal name and the date the will was executed. Never write on, or cross out, sections of your current will. A sample codicil and self-proving certificate are shown in Chapter 5.

The witness procedure for a codicil is the same as that for an original will. The most important point in making sure your will is declared valid is to have it properly witnessed. Your witnesses must be legal adults, must have no interest in the estate, and must attest to your capacity and intent by affixing their signatures in one another's presence to the codicil.

Rewriting Your Will

If you have several changes to make or if your will is not long, you may find it better to rewrite it completely. When you prepare a new will, its first statement includes revocation of all prior wills and codicils. To eliminate any possible confusion, be sure to destroy the original and all copies of your previous will (including any codicils) *after* you have executed your new will.

Keeping Your Will Safe

Your will should always be kept in a safe, secure location, along with other important documents. Always notify your Executor of the location of your will. You may wish to leave your will, or an unsigned copy, with your Executor. Your Executor must have the original document to file with the court when needed.

CAUTION: In some states, the contents of safe deposit boxes are sealed upon the death of the boxholder. If you intend to keep your will in a safe deposit box, be sure to ask your banker about state laws. If the box is sealed, your Executor may not be able to obtain your will quickly when it is needed.

CHAPTER 3

Your Property

Your estate consists of all the property that you personally own. Property consisting of land and any improvements to it is categorized as real property and everything else as personal property. Personal property is further classified as tangible and intangible. Tangible personal property consists of actual items, everything from automobiles and antiques to shoes and socks. Intangible personal property, such as cash, stocks, bonds, and trust share ownership, is representative of value. Intellectual personal property is a form of intangible property and includes copyrights, patents, licenses, and residual performance rights. Both tangible and intangible property may be transferred in your will through individual bequests or as a part of the total estate. In many situations, other estate planning techniques to transfer property, such as joint titling (with right of survivorship), tax-exempt lifetime gifts, or trusts, are more appropriate. Real and personal property, methods of transfer, and related estate planning concerns are discussed in this chapter.

Tangible Personal Property

Your tangible personal property has two components of value, its base cash value and the value of its association with you. Items of one's personal property with little cash value are often treasured by one's loved ones for the positive memories they evoke. Another characteristic of tangible personal property is that its replacement cost generally exceeds its resale value, particularly under forced sale conditions. Almost everyone is aware of the types of bargains available at estate auctions. Recognizing these factors as you review your personal property may prompt additional specific bequests in your will. For example, you may decide that it would be better to give a recently purchased washer and drier or television set to a niece or nephew living nearby rather than to have the items sold and the cash proceeds divided. You also may decide to give keepsake items to those you wish to have them now, when you can personally provide background about their origins and are able to enjoy the giving of the gift. Gifts of tangible personal property made in your will should be specifically identified.

● **Example**

I give my entire collection of U.S. silver dollars, which are kept in my First National Bank of Richmond, Virginia, safe deposit box number 231, to my beloved son, Carl Graham White.

Tangible property includes titled personal property, such as cars, trucks, recreational vehicles, boats, and airplanes. Gifts of such property in your will should be identified by description and title, serial, or I.D. number. You may consider expediting transfer of such personal property by placing it in joint title (with right of survivorship) with your chosen beneficiary. This approach bypasses the probate procedure and may be advantageous for valuable personal property, such as classic automobiles, yachts, and airplanes. Bear in mind that joint titling will require the co-owner's consent if you choose later to sell or exchange the asset involved. Another aspect to consider when reviewing titled personal property is its lien status and how any outstanding balance would be satisfied. If the asset is jointly titled, any liens would become the responsibility of the co-title holder.

Intangible Personal Property

Generally, cash, stocks, bonds, and other financial instruments are considered liquid assets. Liquidity simply refers to the speed with which the value of an asset can be converted into currency without loss. Cash, checking, savings, and money market accounts are highly liquid assets and are often designated to fund monetary bequests. Stocks, bonds, and other financial instruments are readily convertible to cash, although the timing of the conversion is often critical to receiving maximum benefit. Transfer of intangible personal property by arrangements that avoid probate, such as joint titling of accounts or assets with beneficiaries, should be considered as part of your estate plan.

MONETARY GIFTS

When you make monetary bequests in your will, they are deducted from the general assets of your estate after all expenses are paid. If the liquid assets of your estate are insufficient to meet monetary bequests, the Executor may have to sell other real and personal property to fund them. Clearly, the liquidity of your assets is a major consideration when you make specific monetary gifts.

● **Example** ──────────────────────────────

I give my brother, Abraham Lee Light, the sum of $1,000.00.

A gift that is to be paid from a specific source will be paid with funds from the designated source. If the funds from that source are insufficient, and if adequate assets exist in your general estate, the balance may be paid from the general assets. To ensure that your monetary bequests are not reduced or voided, verify that sufficient cash resources are (or will be) available.

● **Example** ──────────────────────────────

I give my sister, Naomi Karen White, the sum of $1,000.00 to be paid from my savings account, #543210, at the 1st National Bank, 101 3rd Street, Salem, Virginia.

If you desire a monetary bequest be used for a specific purpose, be sure to designate the purpose in your bequest.

● **Example** ──────────────────────────────

I give my church, 1st Methodist, 110 Front Street, Richmond, Virginia, the sum of $1,000.00, for the building fund.

Certificates of deposit (CDs), individual retirement accounts (IRAs), and U.S. government savings bonds are somewhat less liquid, since usually they cannot be accessed without penalty (foregone interest and fees) before a specific date. Publicly traded corporate stocks and government and corporate bonds can be highly liquid; however, market fluctuations may make forced sale disadvantageous at certain times. Stock in privately held corporations, limited and regular partnership shares, and private notes are generally the most illiquid forms of commonly held intangible personal property. It is often more beneficial to give intangible personal property directly to your beneficiaries rather than to have it sold to fund monetary bequests.

● **Example**

I give to each of my beloved daughters, Naomi Karen White and Louise Beatrice Hale, 357 shares of my American Telephone and Telegraph (AT&T) preferred stock.

This approach allows the beneficiary to determine the best time to convert the asset into cash. If the beneficiary retains such property for some time, both dividends and fundamental value appreciation may be realized. Often, stock dividends are directed into automatic reinvestments in additional shares. In such a situation, the number of shares and fractional units will be periodically increasing. You may wish your beneficiary to receive the entire amount of stock to prevent the incremental additions from becoming part of your general or residual estate. If this is the case, say so.

● **Example**

I give my grandson, Carroll Abraham Light, II, all of my shares of American Telephone and Telegraph (AT&T) preferred stock.

Bequests of intangible personal property can be for a specific amount, or the assets themselves may be given. For example, you may wish to give the sum of $3,000 to each of your grandchildren, or you may prefer to give each a tax-exempt bond or a certain number of shares of a particular stock. If you choose to make monetary bequests, be sure that you specify how the balance of your intangible personal property is to be distributed. This can be done by leaving your entire estate to one or more primary beneficiary(ies) or a trust, except for the specific monetary bequests. Another option is to make your various bequests and end your will with a residual bequest distributing the remainder to a beneficiary you choose. Since intangible personal property generally increases in value over time as interest and/or dividend payments are received, it is important to arrange for distribution of the entire amount.

INTELLECTUAL PROPERTY

Intellectual property, such as copyrights and patents, can be given to a beneficiary in your will. Intellectual property rights typically have long terms and can be renewed. Fees paid for use of intellectual property are royalties and may constitute a valuable portion of your estate. Intellectual property may be held with another, unrelated person, in which case you may transfer only your interest to your beneficiaries.

● **Example**

I give my wife, Karen Louise Light, my one-half share of patent rights and resultant royalties from the fiberoptic switching system developed with my business associate, Norman James Teller, identified by U.S. Patents G-100689 and G-103746.

It is advisable to refer to the patent or copyright identification number when transferring intellectual property rights. Similarly, if you receive residual payments for television rebroadcast rights, these rights should be clearly identified and given to your chosen beneficiary. Since the value of intellectual property rights is directly related to their use, you should consider leaving special instructions regarding how to maximize their value.

Real Property

Real property consists of land (real estate) and any improvements to or on that land. Real property is characterized by its use. Types of real property include:

Unimproved Property

- Forest
- Range
- Marsh
- Vacant lot

Residential Property

- Primary residence
- Second home
- Lot and mobile home

- Cooperative apartment
- Condominium
- Time-share unit

Income-Producing Property

- Residential
- Farm
- Subdivision
- Campground
- Commercial
    Retail
    Office
    Warehouse
- Industrial
- Hotel
- Marina

The value of each parcel of real property is affected by its location, condition, size, quality, and appropriateness for use. Generally, real property is an appreciating asset, increasing in value over time. Most real property is purchased through a mortgage secured by the property. As the outstanding mortgage balance decreases over time, while the total value of the property usually increases, substantial net equity is gained. Often this equity appreciation in real property value constitutes a significant portion of personal net worth.

When making gifts of real property in your will, be sure to identify specifically the real estate involved. This can be achieved by reference to the street address, including the city and state where the property is located. In cases involving a rural route address or unimproved real estate, it is advisable to identify the subject property by the tax number or lot/tract number. This information, which constitutes a brief legal description of the property, is found in the deed and on property tax bills. Clarity is particularly important when identifying real property owned in a state other than your state of residence.

● **Example** ──

I give my summer home located on Lake Norman, in Mecklenburg County in the state of North Carolina (Tax Map 106, Section 12, Lots 3,4, and 5), to my daughter, Dawn Lee Hale.

──●

DEED OPTIONS

State property laws govern the forms of real estate ownership and deed options available. In many situations, deed options are used to direct the transfer of real property outside the probate process. Titling property so that it automatically transfers to the beneficiary is a common estate planning technique. It is advisable to review real estate deeds to verify the portion and terms of your current ownership interest.

If you are married and live in a community-property state, all property acquired during the marriage is owned by each spouse in equal shares. Property acquired before or outside the marriage, such as an inheritance, is separate property and is owned individually. Community-property interests, if no other provisions are made, must be disposed of in your will.

Joint titling, with right of survivorship, is an option that allows property to transfer without the expense and delay of probate. You may jointly title real property with your spouse or other beneficiary in most states. Tenancy by the entirety, a form of ownership available in some states only to married couples, also transfers property interests to the surviving spouse. The stability of the marriage or of your relationship to the beneficiary should be weighed carefully when planning to title property as joint owners or tenants by the entirety.

If you've titled property so that it transfers automatically, you should also plan for transfer of your estate in the event that you and your spouse or beneficiary die in a common accident or disaster. In these circumstances, your wills, naming an alternate beneficiary for your estates, can dispose of the jointly held property. Because of the possibility of simultaneous death, your will and that of your spouse or other joint owner should agree on alternate beneficiaries. You and your beneficiaries should have a current will at all times to meet this contingency.

Another deed option is the creation of a life estate interest in the property on behalf of a person you choose. A life estate is the right to use the property for the holder's lifetime, separate from ownership, which is listed in the name of another, and is a recorded liability against the property. A life estate is established by amending the property deed.

When planning the transfer of ownership of residential real estate, many factors should be considered. Will your intended beneficiary live in the property? How will any outstanding mortgage balances be paid? Has the property been in your family for a long time? How will maintenance be dealt with? Clearly, the answer to these and similar concerns can change over time. Plans that your spouse and dependent children occupy your large home usually change after your children settle in their own homes. On the other hand, you may have a second residence or vacation home that your family can enjoy for years.

The same considerations apply to condominium and time-share interests in real property. If you have any outstanding mortgage or lien balances secured by the real estate, including home equity lines of credit, further decisions are needed. Should the mortgage(s) and lien(s) be paid off and the property transferred without any encumbrances? Or do you prefer your beneficiary to receive the equity interest and pay the outstanding balance(s) on the existing terms? You must specify your intent and direct your Executor accordingly in your will. Otherwise, the real property may have to be sold to pay outstanding balances, and your beneficiary would realize only the net after sale, quite possibly under distress conditions, yielding less than full value.

INCOME-PRODUCING PROPERTY

Income-producing property should be reviewed in terms of the amount of active involvement required to maintain the income stream. Simple receipt of interest and/or dividends is essentially a passive function that automatically follows the ownership of account, stock, and bond assets. In contrast, ownership of rental property, a farm, or a private business usually requires informed and active management. If your primary beneficiary is not fully involved in, or willing and able to manage, these operations, the income stream may well be diminished or stop altogether.

If you have commercial or rental property that you currently manage, it may be advisable to make separate arrangements for continuing management. Such arrangements are usually contained in a separate document and referenced in your will.

● **Example**

I give my apartment building located at 704–709 Laburnham Avenue in the city of Richmond, Virginia (Tax Number 408-10886), to my son, Charles James Hale, and direct my Executor to give my son, Charles James Hale, my instructions regarding property management contained in a letter of instructions dated June 10, 1989.

When assessing income-producing property that requires active management, you should consider whether it would be better to have the assets sold and the proceeds distributed to your beneficiaries. In such sales, receiving a fair price in your absence may not be possible without adequate preparation. The type of preparation needed will vary depending on the nature of the property or business and the capability of your associates.

For example, if you own commercial real estate that you actively manage, you may need only to locate a suitable agent or firm that can manage the property, with the ownership and income stream passing to your beneficiaries. As the current owner/manager, you are best qualified to select an agent, based on your own local knowledge. You should discuss your intentions with your prospective agent and obtain a binding agreement fixing the agent's terms of compensation. This agreement should be immediately available to your Executor, with careful guidance set forth in your letter of instructions. You may further provide suggestions as to property value and indicate a strategy to sell your property over a period of years, based on market value and tax considerations. Income-producing property may involve a basic break-even income/expense position while awaiting future sale at appreciated value. In such situations, purchase of additional life insurance to provide for payment of obligations can minimize the risk of loss.

Business and farm operations usually require special arrangements for continuing management. If you actively manage a farm or closely held business, finding a suitable replacement manager is apt to be difficult. If a member of your family has the desire to continue operating the business or farm, that person should be brought into the daily operations as soon as is practicable. If, on the other hand, none of your beneficiaries has the desire or ability to maintain operations, other arrangements will be required. Buy–sell agreements and installment sales are practical options for such transfers.

Life Insurance

At some stages, review of your net property position may show a shortfall of asset value relative to total liens and liabilities. This can happen even when you have substantial net worth if your primary assets consist of real property or a private business concern. Potential cash shortfall can be covered by life insurance policies to prevent forced sale of real estate and business assets (often at a deep discount). Life insurance can be viewed as contingent intangible personal property. Life insurance policies have owners and name beneficiaries, and their proceeds do not pass through the probate process unless they are payable to the estate of the decedent or to the Executor. Mortgage balance and credit card balance insurance are examples of life insurance that is paid on behalf of the estate and pass through probate. A life insurance policy on the life of another person is considered the property of the policy owner and is valued at the replacement value of the policy.

After making an inventory of your personal property, both tangible and intangible, and identifying your liens and liabilities, you should easily be able to figure your net position. A series of property inventory sheets is included in the Records set for this purpose.

CHAPTER *4*

Bequests and Special Instructions

The primary purpose of your will is to set out plans and instructions for your estate. As the sample will in the Introduction illustrates, a will can be very short and direct. Your will can also be a creative document, outlining plans for individual items of your estate, and you may, if you wish, include terms of endearment. The number and type of instructions and bequests in your will should be decided carefully. Before you begin the actual process of writing a will, make a list of beneficiaries and bequests, with correct names and adequate descriptions of gifts. Documents or other records to be listed in your will should be noted by date or reference number. Your chosen Executor and others who have key roles in your plans should be informed and agree to appointment. Other preparation needed to write a will depends on your personal situation and goals. The "execution" of your will requires at least two witnesses (three in Louisiana and Vermont) to see you actually sign and date the document. If you wish to self-prove your will, you and your witnesses must appear before a notary public. Make any necessary arrangements for witnesses or self-proving in advance.

A variety of bequests and special instructions that may be made regarding the disposition of property are illustrated in this chapter. Plan carefully and review your estate, beneficiaries, and goals before beginning to write your bequests.

Language in Your Will

The language you use when writing bequests or other provisions is critical to establishing *intent* and can affect the way your estate is distributed. When writing your will, you should always use direct, easily understandable language. Words that do *not* specifically indicate your intentions can cause confusion when your will is probated. Words such as "wish," "want," "hope," "believe," and other predicatory words only suggest your intentions rather than stating them, and therefore may not be legally binding, as in the following statement.

● Unclear Intent

I *wish* my nephew, Charles James Hale, to have my 1939 Chevrolet, SN 12345.

Although this statement may indicate that it is your *desire* that your nephew have the car, there is no clear statement of your *intent* that he have it. A clear statement follows.

● Clear Intent

I *give* my 1939 Chevrolet, SN 12345, to my nephew, Charles James Hale.

The use of simple, direct language helps ensure that your estate plan is followed. There is no requirement that you use legal terms or phrases or fancy words; just be sure that your intent is obvious by stating it clearly and simply. Including terms of endearment or explanation when writing your bequests is a matter of personal choice. Stating your relationship to the beneficiary in the bequest helps make the identity obvious and avoids confusion.

Do not use the term "heir(s)" in your will. An heir is any person who might be entitled to a portion of your estate if you were to die intestate, that is, without a valid will. The rules of intestate succession vary from state to state and, hence, so do possible heirs. The term "beneficiary" is appropriate when referring to those whom you wish to receive a portion of your estate under your will.

If you have a previous will, it may contain legal terms or phrases that are unfamiliar to you. Keep in mind that a will can convey your wishes only if you completely understand its contents. Two common phrases found in wills are *per stirpes* and *per capita,* both of which refer to methods of distribution.

Per stirpes (literally, "by the roots") means distribution to descendants. Be aware that *per stirpes* distribution applies to your *direct* descendants only, that is, children, grandchildren, and great-grandchildren. A bequest to one of your children made *per stirpes* would be distributed to that child's children if your child is not alive when your will is probated. If that child had no surviving children (issue), the share would be distributed equally among your other descendants.

● **Example**

I give my farmland in Botetourt County, Virginia, Parcels 104-1178, 101-4712, and 104-118, to my three beloved children, Abraham Lee Light, Naomi Karen White, and Louise Beatrice Hale, in equal shares, per stirpes.

Per capita ("by head") means equal distribution to those named. In *per capita* distribution, only those named who are living at the time the will is presented for probate will share equally. If you direct that your estate be distributed to your children on a *per capita* basis, and one of your children named did not survive you, their descendants (if any) would receive nothing, and their share would be equally distributed to the other named beneficiaries. If, however, you direct that your estate be distributed *per capita* to "issue" surviving you, then your estate would be divided equally among all your living descendants, children, grandchildren, and great-grandchildren.

When writing your will, choose your words carefully so that your intent is clear. Specific identification of people and property and direct phrasing of instructions are the keys to clarity. Your will should be written so that it is simple to understand and not subject to misinterpretation. Keeping your will current also helps to make it simple and clear.

Evaluating Your Estate

As discussed in Chapter 3, preparing a will usually begins with making an inventory of the property and assets of your estate. A careful review of real and personal property can reveal assets that have special significance and value to you and your beneficiaries. Real property that has been passed from generation to generation can have value to family members far beyond its monetary worth. The history and memories associated with land and homes often provide a family with a sense of unity, linking past, present, and future generations. Continuity of family ownership of such property can be important when you choose your beneficiaries.

Family history is often tied to items of personal property as well. Jewelry, antiques, household items, and other personal property can have a history of ownership spanning several generations. Although often overlooked, gifts of personal items can be of immense value to the beneficiaries who receive them. Carefully review the origins and significance of all personal property when making an inventory. A description of the item and its place in the history of your family can make it a treasure of great worth to the beneficiary.

After making an inventory of the property you intend to give, you must decide who will receive the gift. The health, age, and location of your beneficiaries may affect the way you write your will. If, for instance, a beneficiary is unable to drive, a gift of a car will have little value. You may ask your intended beneficiaries if certain personal or household items would be of special value or interest to them. Carefully consider situations that may involve a division of property between beneficiaries. Disagreements may be prevented by detailing, either by prior discussion or in your will, the manner in which property should be divided. If beneficiaries live in distant locations, the cost of transporting items such as large household goods may be prohibitive.

Note your plans for beneficiaries who are minors or not mature enough to be entrusted with a gift, either cash or other personal property. The safekeeping of such gifts may be entrusted to a relative or, in the case of cash, distributed through other methods, such as a trust. Decisions regarding charitable bequests should include the amount of the gift and the purpose for which it is to be used. The full names and addresses of beneficiaries, along with a description of gifts, can be especially useful to your Executor in the probate process.

Identifying Beneficiaries and Bequests

When making gifts of personal property, it is very important to identify fully the gift and the beneficiary. Without adequate identification, confusion may result when your will is probated.

● **Unclear**

I give my ring to my nephew, Charles.

Which ring? How many nephews named Charles are there? You can easily avoid problems of this type by carefully identifying the gift and the beneficiary.

● **Clear**

I give my gold Masonic ring, inscribed A.L.L., to my nephew, Charles James Hale.

Obviously, the more bequests and beneficiaries you have, the more important identification becomes. Never rely on a single name or a vague description to identify your beneficiaries or bequests.

● **Unclear**

I give my entire estate to my cousins in equal shares.

Such a statement may result in the probate court defining the term "cousin" to mean all the people who fall in a strict legal interpretation of that term. First cousins, second cousins, third cousins, cousins you did not realize you had!

● **Unclear**

I give my entire estate to my children, in equal shares.

Similarly, the preceding statement means *all* your children, by previous marriage(s), illegitimate, and otherwise. Be very careful to name each beneficiary. Never describe a beneficiary or a group of beneficiaries in general terms.

Bequests

Generally, there are no limitations on your ability to leave your estate to whomever you desire. Exceptions to this right to dispose of your property may apply if you are married. Some states grant a "dower" or "curtsey" right to a surviving spouse. Such a right determines a minimum amount of an estate the surviving spouse is entitled to. Louisiana, in addition to maintaining spousal rights, requires that a Testator not totally disinherit his or her children.

Another restriction on your freedom to dispose of your estate as you wish applies to conditional bequests. Conditional bequests that require a beneficiary to act in an unreasonable manner or to do something irrational or illegal to receive his or her bequest should be avoided. If a condition is illegal or against public policy, the court may choose to ignore it and grant the bequest. If a beneficiary objects to the condition, he or she may simply refuse the bequest. The condition, and the method of determining when and if it is satisfied, must be set out. Conditional bequests usually result in your estate's being kept open until the conditions are met and may require extensive time and effort on the part of your Executor. If controlling the actions of your beneficiaries is a vital concern, you should consider a trust or other arrangements.

If you make a bequest of personal property, such as a specific automobile, and later sell or dispose of the car, it is obviously not a part of your estate. Property that no longer exists in your estate when your will is probated is "adeemed" and, therefore, the beneficiary cannot receive it. When a bequest is adeemed, that particular bequest fails, although the other terms of the will are not affected.

If you leave monetary gifts in excess of the assets of your estate, those gifts may be "abated." This simply means that each beneficiary's share is reduced proportionally.

● Example

I give my sons, Samuel Gordon Stull and Paul Leslie Stull, the sum of $100,000.00 each.

If, after all debts, taxes, and funeral expenses are settled, only $150,000 remained of the Testator's estate, each son would receive $75,000.

CONTINGENT BEQUESTS

At many times in life, a single beneficiary is named to receive the entire estate of the Testator.

● Example

I give my entire estate to my beloved wife, Naomi Lee Spencer Light.

This simple bequest is direct, easy to understand, and fully identifies the beneficiary. The "entire estate" includes *all* the real and personal property owned by the Testator at the time of death. A person who receives the entire estate of the Testator is known as the "sole beneficiary." Although this bequest is complete, it makes no provisions for the distribution of the estate if the sole beneficiary were to die at the same time or soon before the Testator. Naming a contingent beneficiary to receive the bequest, in case the Testator and primary beneficiary die at the same time, is extremely important.

● Example

I give my entire estate to my wife, Naomi Lee Spencer Light, if she survives me by 180 days. If she does not survive me by 180 days, then I give my entire estate to my son, Abraham Lee Light.

In this bequest, the Testator has clearly stated that his spouse must survive him by six months in order to receive that bequest. This can prevent the estate from being transferred prematurely and can provide tax advantages if the estate is substantial.

Many times, bequests are made "contingent" on the beneficiary outliving the testator by a specified amount of time.

● Example

I give my son, Abraham Lee Light, my Parker shotgun, SN 456789, if he survives me by 180 days.

If the son died less than six months after the Testator, the bequest would fail, and the property would revert to the general estate. Many states require by law that beneficiaries named in a will survive the Testator by at least 5–30 days. A beneficiary who does not live the amount of time specified by law or in the will is considered to have predeceased the Testator, and the bequest is not distributed but remains a part of the general or residual estate.

You may also name a *contingent,* or alternate, beneficiary to receive the gift when you make a bequest.

● Example

I give my sister, Louise Beatrice Hale, my diamond dinner ring, inscribed N.K.L. If she does not survive me, then I give the ring to my niece, Dawn Lee Hale.

In this situation, the sister will receive the ring if she survives the Testator; if not, the niece will be the beneficiary. By naming an alternate beneficiary, you can be sure that someone you choose will receive a specific item or asset.

It is especially important for married people to designate an alternate beneficiary.

● Example

I give all my estate to my wife, Rachel Beatrice Stull. If she does not survive me by 180 days, then I give my estate, in equal shares, to my cousin, Gordon Leslie Stull, and the Pennsylvania Baptist Children's Home, Inc., Hershey, Pennsylvania.

In the preceding example, if the Testator and his spouse were to die in a common accident, there would be no question of his intent that the estate be divided equally between his alternate beneficiaries.

Care taken in planning your bequests can ensure that your estate is distributed to the beneficiaries you choose.

RESIDUAL BEQUESTS

Anything left of your estate after your property is distributed by the terms of your will is known as the residue of your estate. If you have directed the disposition of *all* your property, there will be no residue.

● **Example**

I give my *entire* estate to my sons, Samuel Gordon Stull and Paul Leslie Stull, in equal shares.

In this example, the will disposes of the *entire* estate of the Testator. Therefore, no residue remains in the estate.

If you've disposed of your *entire* estate in your will, there is no need for a residual bequest. Those who have disposed of their estate by individual bequests may have a residual estate. A bequest of property that is not distributed becomes part of your residual estate.

● **Example**

I give my sons, Samuel Gordon Stull and Paul Leslie Stull, the sum of $50,000.00 each.

Suppose that after all expenses are paid and the $50,000 bequest is fulfilled, $10,000 remains in the Testator's estate. A residual bequest allows the Testator to provide for anything left of the estate.

● **Example**

I give my sons, Samuel Gordon Stull and Paul Leslie Stull, the sum of $50,000.00 each. I give all the residue of my estate to the American Cancer Society, 101 First Street, Los Angeles, California.

If you intend to make a residual bequest, be sure to consider your situation carefully, since the actual amount of the residue of your estate may be more than you planned. If there is no residual estate, then the residual bequest will have no effect. Conversely, the residual estate could become significantly larger than anticipated. In the preceding example, if the Testator had bought an airline ticket with a credit card that automatically issued life insurance and if the plane crashed, killing the Testator, the residue of his estate would be increased by the amount of the life insurance issued. Assuming that the policy paid out $200,000 to the estate, the residue would change from $10,000 to $210,000, all of which would go to the charity named. Clearly, the Testator had not actually intended the charity to receive more than his sons; yet this is what would happen.

CHARITABLE BEQUESTS

The same care and thought given to other gifts should be applied to charitable bequests. It's particularly important to identify the charity or organization by full name and address, as many charities, churches, and organizations have similar names.

● **Example**

I give the sum of $500.00 to the American Heart Foundation, located at 415 Melrose Avenue, Los Angeles, California.

The purpose of your charitable bequest may also be designated.

● **Example**

I give Brooklyn College, Brooklyn, New York, the sum of $500.00, for the library fund.

Many colleges and charitable institutions provide assistance for those who wish to make a gift. If you are considering a substantial bequest, discuss the gift with a representative of the beneficiary organization. Such organizations often employ estate planning personnel to assist contributors with tax-advantageous methods of giving. Charitable bequests, like all other provisions included in your will, should be reviewed periodically for accuracy and applicability.

Special Instructions

Provisions and instructions are included in a will to address the personal needs and goals of the Testator. You may include any legal, reasonable instructions regarding the disposition of your estate in your will. Keep in mind that the probate court cannot add to, or delete from, the instructions you have made concerning your estate. For this reason, it is always wise to make any instructions direct, complete, and to the point. Be sure to consider fully the intended result of any instructions to be sure that they will have the effect you desire. Never include an unneeded or irrelevant instruction that could be misinterpreted and could conflict with other terms of your will. The same cautions that apply when wording bequests apply to instructions in your will. Avoid the use of vague or contradictory terms, and be sure your intentions are stated clearly.

● **Example** ────────────────────────────────────

I direct my Executor to arrange that I be buried in the Light family cemetery located near the community of Fincastle, Virginia, on Rural Route 625-E.

──●

This provision is clear in its purpose and language. The Testator directed the Executor to arrange burial in the family cemetery; the description is adequate, and the intent is plain. The directions of the Testator would be followed, assuming that the will was readily available and that the Executor acted quickly. Provisions included in your will that are time-sensitive, such as burial instructions, may not be followed if your will is not immediately available to your Executor or alternate. When including provisions of this type, be sure to inform your Executor of your plans.

A provision in your will may be set out to specify the length of time beneficiaries must survive you in order to receive bequests.

● **Example** ────────────────────────────────────

If any beneficiary named in this, my last will, does not survive me by 180 days, then that beneficiary shall be deemed to have predeceased me.

──●

Any beneficiary named in this will *must* survive the Testator by the length of time stated before the bequest is distributed. The purpose of setting out a provision such as this is to ensure that a gift won't be made to a person who dies very soon after the Testator and therefore would get no real benefit from, or use of, the bequest. The gift would revert to the estate of the Testator and therefore be available to be distributed by the Testator's will. If no provision were made, and the beneficiary died suddenly after the Testator, the bequest would become a part of the estate of the beneficiary. You may state the time a beneficiary must survive you in each bequest or make a provision regarding all beneficiaries in a single provision.

Provisions can be used to set out your plans for resolving any disagreements that may arise over the way your estate is divided.

● **Example**

I direct my Executor to fairly settle any disagreement that may arise over the division of my furniture and household goods, which I have left in equal shares to my son, Abraham Lee Light, and my daughter, Mary Alice Light.

The Executor is clearly instructed to settle any controversy that may occur regarding the division of the Testator's furniture or other household goods. Rather than directing, and listing, every item individually, the Testator had given this bequest in equal shares and named the Executor to settle any disagreements.

Special instructions are often included in a will to provide for the welfare and disposition of pets.

● **Example**

I direct my Executor to find caring homes for my two dogs, Bruno and Otis. Any reasonable expenses incurred while finding new homes for them is to be paid from my estate.

The Executor of this estate is directed to find homes for the two dogs and is authorized to incur reasonable expenses for boarding, food, and other costs. This example illustrates the detail you may include when writing special instructions or provisions.

You may set out compensation for your Executor in your will.

● **Example**

I give my Executor, Thomas Lee Smith, the sum of $2,000.00 in appreciation of his efforts on my behalf in settling my estate.

Remember, there is usually no reason to compensate an Executor who is a primary beneficiary beyond the gifts made in your will. To do so means that your Executor's (beneficiary's) share of the estate, like that of other beneficiaries, will be reduced by the amount specified for the Executor. Your Executor will have to report any compensation as personal income. Also, be aware that all states set out an amount, usually expressed as a percent (3 to 5 percent) of the value of the estate or "reasonable compensation" that an Executor may claim for acting on your behalf. If you have named an Executor who is not a beneficiary and have specified as compensation an amount that is substantially less than the courts deem appropriate, the Executor may petition the court for the higher amount allowed by law.

Your will may include a provision stating that if any beneficiary of your will should contest the will, that beneficiary is to receive nothing. This "no contest" provision is known as an *in terrorem* clause. If an *in terrorem* clause relates to a conditional bequest, it may not be accepted by the probate court. Usually, an *in terrorem* clause is included to reinforce the intent of the Testator who has reason to anticipate a challenge to the will.

CHAPTER 5

A Family and Its Estate: A Story with Sample Documents

This story of the fictitious Light family traces the growth of the Light family estate from the beginning of the twentieth century. Completed wills and related documents appear at the end of the story to illustrate how this family transferred its property from generation to generation.

NOTE: The signature and witness block has been omitted from the sample wills in this chapter to save space. All testamentary wills must be signed and witnessed according to state requirements.

The Light Family at the Turn of the Century

Brandy Run Farm was established in Botetourt County, Virginia, by Paul Samuel Light in 1896. Paul Samuel Light's will, which was probated after his death in 1933, appears in the Introduction.

Paul's son, Carroll Abraham Light, first opened his eyes to the twentieth century at Brandy Run Farm on January 2, 1900. He and his family would be touched by three wars in the next 90 years.

Remembering

In 1988, Abraham Lee Light, Carroll's son, was called on to settle his mother's estate. He was 53 years old. He and his aunt, Mary Alice Light, were now the senior members of the Light family. Brandy Run, the family farm, established before the turn of the century by his grandfather, Paul Samuel Light, was prosperous. His father, Carroll Abraham Light, and Mary Alice had both been born there. In time, Mary Alice would see her last mountain sunset from the old south porch. His own grandchildren were just discovering the fun of playing next to the small stream, Brandy Run. He felt the continuity and stability his family took from the land.

1900–1920

Light Family Key Dates

Date	Name	Event	Location
1900	Carroll Abraham Light	Born	Brandy Run Farm, Virginia
1907	Nathaniel Benjamin Greene Louise Karen Connor	Married	New York, New York
1908	Rachel Beatrice Greene	Born	Tarrytown, New York
1909	Louise Connor Greene	Born	Tarrytown, New York
1910	Mary Alice Light	Born	Brandy Run Farm, Virginia
1912	Karen Louise Greene	Born	Tarrytown, New York
*1918	Carroll Abraham Light	World War I	France

*Will sample related to event shown.

Abraham looked through the file of family documents he had assembled from his mother's papers. The simple holographic will his father had written in 1918, leaving everything to his sister, Mary Alice, prior to shipping out to France in the last days of World War I, impressed him with its maturity. (See Figure 3.)

Being of sound mind, I hereby write my Last Will and Testament. I give my entire estate to my dear sister, Mary Alice Light, and appoint my father, Paul Samuel Light, as my Executor.

Carroll Abraham Light
May 13, 1918
Norfolk, Virginia

Figure 3

1920–1940

Light Family Key Dates

Date	Name	Event	Location
1920	Carroll Abraham Light		
	June Susan Eaton	Married	Bedford County, Virginia
1921	Samuel Paul Light	Born	Bedford County, Virginia
1927	June Susan Eaton	Leaves	Texas
1928	Carroll Abraham Light	Divorced	Bedford County, Virginia
1929	Louise Connor Greene		
	George Walter Larson	Married	Tarrytown, New York
1929	Susan Elizabeth Larson	Born	Tarrytown, New York
1930	Rachel Beatrice Greene		
	Samuel Grice Stull	Married	Tarrytown, New York
1930	Karen Louise Greene	College	Hollins, Virginia
1932	Charlene Ruth Larson	Born	Tarrytown, New York
*1933	Paul Samuel Light	Died	Brandy Run Farm, Virginia
1934	Carroll Abraham Light		
	Karen Louise Greene	Married	Tarrytown, New York
1936	Abraham Lee Light	Born	Alhambra, California
1939	Naomi Karen Light	Born	Alhambra, California

*Will sample related to event shown in Introduction.

After his return from Europe, Carroll Light married June Susan Eaton of Bedford County, Virginia; in 1921, they had a son, Samuel Paul Light. Six years later, June deserted Carroll and Samuel and moved to Texas. Subsequently, Carroll enrolled in college, taking engineering courses. His parents helped with young Sam.

Carroll divorced June and, four years later, met Karen Louise Greene, who was then starting her junior year at Hollins College, majoring in English. Karen was from Tarrytown, New York, and was the youngest of the three daughters of Nathaniel Benjamin Greene and his wife, the former Louise Karen Connor. Karen's father, Nathaniel, had taken over his father's clothing manufacturing business in Brooklyn, and the family lived well.

Louise Connor Greene ("Connie") was the first of the Greene sisters to marry. She wed George Walter Larson, a jazz musician, in February 1929. In September of 1929, Karen's niece, Susan Elizabeth Larson, was born. The following year, Karen's other sister, Rachel, married Samuel Grice Stull, a banker from Philadelphia. Abraham's mother's eyes had sparkled whenever she recalled the summers in Tarrytown and the gala weddings of her sisters.

In 1932, Connie had another daughter, Charlene Ruth Larson, and, shortly thereafter, Karen met Carroll and his son, Sam. Even though Karen had never thought of starting her family with a teenage son, and despite the reservations of Carroll's father, Karen and Carroll became engaged. Carroll's father died of a heart attack the day after Christmas in 1933, and Karen and her future mother-in-law, Naomi Lee Light, became close.

After her graduation from Hollins in the spring of 1934, Karen and Carroll were married in Tarrytown, New York. Next, the new family moved to Alhambra, California, and Carroll started working as an engineer for Hughes Aircraft. Abraham was born on March 15, 1936, and his sister, Naomi Karen Light, was born in 1939. Abraham had only the vaguest memories of his half-brother, Sam, who joined the Navy later that year.

1940–1960

Light Family Key Dates

Date	Name	Event	Location
1941	Samuel Paul Light	Died	Pearl Harbor, Hawaii
1942	Louise Beatrice Light	Born	Alhambra, California
1945	Nathaniel Benjamin Greene	Died	Miami, Florida
1950	Karen Louise (Connor) Greene	Died	Miami, Florida
*1954	Naomi Lee (Spencer) Light	Died	Brandy Run Farm, Virginia
1957	Abraham Lee Light		
	Susan Linda Anthony	Married	Fincastle, Virginia
1958	Carroll Abraham Light, II	Born	Salem, Virginia

*Will sample related to event shown.

Samuel Paul Light was killed in the Japanese attack on Pearl Harbor on December 7, 1941. His father's copy of Sam's will was in the file; Sam had left everything to his baby half-sister, Naomi. His father started a college fund for her with the proceeds. Abraham's other sister, Louise Beatrice Light, was born in 1942. Carroll was promoted, and when Abraham was eight, the Light family moved to a larger house in Alhambra.

Karen's father, Nathaniel, sold his business in 1943, and he and his wife, Louise, moved to Miami, Florida. After only two years of retirement, Nathaniel died. He had wisely invested the proceeds from the sale of his business and left a substantial trust, which provided Louise with a generous income until she died in Miami in 1950. (See Figure 4.) After her mother's death, Karen received a one-third interest in the trust, as did her two sisters. Except for trips to Florida, the years after the war were quiet as Karen raised her children and began a career as a free-lance writer.

Abraham's father was 54 when he moved his family back to Brandy Run Farm in Botetourt County, Virginia, following the death of his mother, Naomi Lee Light. Abraham's grandmother was buried in the family cemetery at Brandy Run, as were all the Lights except Samuel. Years later, as Abraham settled his mother's estate, he would remember this time when his father faced a similar duty.

As Carroll became involved in improving Brandy Run, Abraham took agriculture courses at Virginia Polytechnic Institute, where his father had earned his engineering degree. In June of 1957, Abraham married Susan Linda Anthony at the Fincastle Presbyterian Church, and they settled in Salem, Virginia. Abraham worked with his father improving the dairy operation and expanding the apple orchards at Brandy Run while Susan taught elementary school. Carroll bought his sister's share of Brandy Run, but Mary Alice, who never married, continued to live there.

On December 18, 1958, Abraham's son, Carroll Abraham Light, II, was born. Karen, now a grandmother, enjoyed the tranquility at the farm and the companionship of Mary Alice, as her husband and son worked together, and she tended young Carroll.

1960–1980

Light Family Key Dates

Date	Name	Event	Location
1963	Naomi Karen Light		
	Robert William Cotswold	Married	Madison, Wisconsin
1964	Karen Beth Cotswold	Born	Madison, Wisconsin
1964	Louise Beatrice Light		
	Frederick Roger Hale	Married	Brandy Run Farm, Virginia
1965	Samuel Grice Stull	Died	Philadelphia, Pennsylvania

(*continued*)

Light Family Key Dates (continued)

Date	Name	Event	Location
1965	Charles James Hale	Born	Charlottesville, Virginia
*1967	Rachel Beatrice (Greene) Stull	Died	Philadelphia, Pennsylvania
1968	Dawn Lee Hale	Born	Charlottesville, Virginia
1969	Robert William Cotswold	Died	Vietnam
1972	Naomi Karen (Light) Cotswold Graham Carl White	Married	Richmond, Virginia

*Will sample related to event shown.

Karen's daughter, Naomi, had finished her studies at the University of Wisconsin when she met and married Robert William Cotswold, a career Army officer, in 1963. Karen's first grandaughter, Karen Beth Cotswold, was born in Madison, Wisconsin, the following year. Also in 1964, Karen's younger daughter, Louise, married Frederick Roger Hale at Brandy Run in an outdoor ceremony. The coupled settled near Charlottesville, where Fred operated an automobile dealership and Charles James Hale, Abraham's nephew, was born in 1965.

Reviewing the file, Abraham read through his mother's copy of her sister's will. (See Figures 5 and 6.) Rachel Beatrice Stull, who died in 1967, had no children, and her husband had died two years earlier. Karen, as Rachel's Executor, had settled her estate and received a substantial bequest.

Abraham's second niece, Dawn Lee Hale, was born in Charlottesville in 1968. War intruded on the Light family again in 1969, when Naomi's husband, Robert William Cotswold, was killed in Vietnam. Abraham's sister stayed in Madison, Wisconsin, and, in 1970, named Abraham as contingent Executor and guardian for her daughter, Karen Beth Cotswold. Abraham was glad that Naomi prepared a new will soon after her remarriage in 1972. (See Figure 7.) Naomi and Graham Carl White subsequently moved to Richmond, Virginia.

1980–1990

Light Family Key Dates

Date	Name	Event	Location
1980	Carroll Abraham Light, II Jo Anne Stone	Married	Dallas, Texas
1982	Louise Connor (Greene) Larson	Died	Tarrytown, New York

(continued)

Light Family Key Dates (continued)

Date	Name	Event	Location
1984	Linda Lee Light	Born	Salem, Virginia
1984	Carroll Abraham Light	Died	Brandy Run Farm, Virginia
*1987	Paul Abraham Light	Born	Salem, Virginia
*1988	Karen Louise (Greene) Light	Died	Provo, Utah
**1989	IRS Form 706 for Estate of Karen Louise Light filed by Abraham Lee Light, Executor.		
*1989	Carroll Abraham Light, II	New will	Salem, Virginia
*1989	Jo Anne Stone Light	New will	Salem, Virginia
1990	Abraham Lee Light	New will	Salem, Virginia
1990	Susan Anthony Light	New will	Salem, Virginia

*Will sample related to event shown.
**Sample IRS Form 706 appears in Chapter 8.

It was in July 1980 that Abraham and Susan's son, Carroll Abraham Light, II, married Jo Anne Stone. Abraham and Susan helped the newlyweds buy a house just down the street. In 1982, Abraham's aunt, Connie Larson, died in her hometown, Tarrytown, New York.

On April 28, 1984, Abraham became a grandfather when Linda Lee Light was born. Both of Abraham's parents were delighted with their first great-granddaughter. In December, Abraham's father, Carroll, died in his sleep, and Abraham helped his mother settle the estate.

Abraham encouraged his mother to buy a new Mercedes and to travel. On July 11, 1987, his mother's first great-grandson, Paul Abraham Light, was born in Salem. (See Figures 8 and 9.) The following year, as Abraham drove his mother to Dulles Airport, he had no way of knowing that her long-planned trip to Hawaii would end tragically in a field in Utah. (See Figures 10 through 13.)

The process that Abraham followed in settling his mother's estate is outlined in the Executor's Checklist in Chapter 6, and a sample of the U.S. Estate Tax Return for the estate is provided in Chapter 8.

LAST WILL AND TESTAMENT

I, *Naomi Lee Spencer Light*, resident
of the *County* of *Botetourt* in the State of *Virginia* ,
being of sound mind, do make and declare the following to be my LAST WILL AND TESTAMENT
and expressly revoke all my prior wills and codicils and certify that I am not acting under undue
influence, duress or menace.

I. EXECUTOR

I appoint *Abraham Lee Light, my son,* EXECUTOR
of this my LAST WILL AND TESTAMENT. If this EXECUTOR is unable to serve for any reason,
then I appoint *Mary Alice Light, my Daughter,* EXECUTOR.
The EXECUTOR is empowered to carry out all provisions of this WILL.
The EXECUTOR shall have all statutory powers available under State law.
The EXECUTOR named shall not be required to post surety bond. I direct that no outside appraisal
be made of my estate, unless required for estate tax purposes.

II. BEQUESTS

I give my entire estate to my dear son, Abraham Lee Light, and to my beloved daughter, Mary Alice Light, in equal shares. This concludes my Last Will and Testament.

Figure 4

LAST WILL AND TESTAMENT

I, _____ Rachel Beatrice Stull _____ , resident
of the _____ City _____ of _____ Philadelphia _____ in the State of __PENNSYLVANIA__,
being of sound mind, do make and declare the following to be my LAST WILL AND TESTAMENT
and expressly revoke all my prior wills and codicils and certify that I am not acting under undue
influence, duress or menace.

I. EXECUTOR

I appoint _____ Karen Louise Light, my sister, _____ EXECUTOR
of this, my LAST WILL AND TESTAMENT. If this EXECUTOR is unable to serve for any reason,
then I appoint _____ Abraham Lee Light, my nephew _____ EXECUTOR.
The EXECUTOR is empowered to carry out all provisions of this WILL.
The EXECUTOR shall have all statutory powers available under State law.
The EXECUTOR named shall not be required to post surety bond.
I direct that no outside appraisal be made of my estate, unless
required for estate tax purposes.

II. BEQUESTS

I give my house, located at 115 Oak Park Drive in the City of
Philadephia, Pennsylvania, to my sister, Louise Connor Larson.

I give my winter home, located at 2120 Key Biscayne Boulevard
in the City of Miami, Florida, to my sister Louise Connor
Larson.

I give all household items, excepting my jewelry and silver
service, to my sister, Louise Connor Larson.

If my sister, Louise Connor Larson, does not survive me by 180
days, then I give her bequests to her daughters, my nieces,
Susan Elizabeth Reynolds and Charlene Ruth Brown, in equal
shares.

I give Mary Ann Washington, my housekeeper, companion and
friend, the sum of five thousand dollars ($5,000.00) and request
that she provide a home for my cats, Ermine and Silky, as we
discussed together.

I give the sum of ten thousand dollars ($10,000.00) to Hunter
College in Queens, New York to the Library Fund for purchase
of art books.

Figure 5

63

I give the sum of five thousand dollars ($5,000.00) to the Philadelphia Art Museum, 608 Main Street, Philadelphia, Pennsylvania for the general purposes of the organization.

I give my church, Westminister Presbyterian Church, 18 Society Hill Place, Philadelphia, Pennsylvania the sum of ten thousand dollars ($10,000.00).

I give the American Cancer Society, 1026 Fifth Avenue, New York, New York the sum of ten thousand dollars ($10,000.00) for the purpose of continuing cancer research.

I give my jewelry and silver services to my beloved sister, Karen Louise Light. I give all the rest of my entire estate, except for the above specific bequests, to my sister, Karen Louise Light, including my one third ownership in the NBG 30 year trust established November 6, 1945, and all cash and securities.

If my sister Karen Louise Light, does not survive me by 180 days, then I give her bequests to her children, Abraham Lee Light, Naomi Karen Cotswold and Louise Beatrice Hale, in equal shares, per stirpes.

This ends my Last Will and Testament

Figure 6

LAST WILL AND TESTAMENT

I, _____ Naomi Karen Cotswold _____ , resident

of the ___ City ___ of ___ Madison ___ in the State of ___ WISCONSIN ___ ,

being of sound mind, do make and declare the following to be my LAST WILL AND TESTAMENT and expressly revoke all my prior wills and codicils and certify that I am not acting under undue influence, duress or menace.

I. EXECUTOR

I appoint _____ Louise Beatrice Hale, my sister, _____ EXECUTOR of this my LAST WILL AND TESTAMENT. If this EXECUTOR is unable to serve for any reason,

then I appoint _____ Abraham Lee Light, my brother, _____ EXECUTOR.

The EXECUTOR is empowered to carry out all provisions of this WILL.

The EXECUTOR shall have all statutory powers available under State law.

The EXECUTOR named shall not be required to post surety bond. I direct that no outside appraisal be made of my estate, unless required for estate tax purposes.

I direct that my Executor see that I am buried in the Light family cemetery located on Brandy Run Farm, in Botetourt County, Virginia.

II. BEQUESTS

I give my entire estate to my beloved daughter, Karen Beth Cotswold, with the exception of the following three bequests.

1. To my dear sister, Louise Beatrice Hale, I give my diamond and sapphire dinner ring.

2. To my dear brother, Abraham Lee Light, I give my 1965 Ford Mustang Convertible, SN-Q4697216-K.

3. I give the sum of five hundred dollars ($500.00) to my church, Saint James Episcopal Church, 117 Shady Lane, Madison, Wisconsin.

I direct my Executor to be certain that my life insurance policy proceeds fund the trust to be administered by the First Bank and Trust Company of Madison, Wisconsin, in accord with the trust agreement, dated April 15, 1970.

I appoint my sister, Louise Beatrice Hale, as guardian of my daughter, Karen Beth Cotswold, until she attains her majority. If my sister, Louise Beatrice Hale, does not survive me, then I appoint my brother Abraham Lee Light, as guardian of my daughter, Karen Beth Cotswold, until she attains her majority.

This concludes this my Last Will and Testament.

Figure 7

CODICIL

I, _____ Abraham Lee Light _____ , resident

of the ___ City ___ of _____ Salem _____ in the State of

___ VIRGINIA ___ , being of sound mind, do make and declare this codicil to

be my LAST WILL AND TESTAMENT dated _____ June 26 _____ , 19 _85_ and

certify that I am not acting under undue influence, duress or menace.

I hereby add this additional specific bequest:

I give to my grandson, Paul Abraham Light, the sum of five
thousand dollars ($5,000.00).

In all other respects I ratify and confirm my Will and in witness whereof, I have hereunto set

my hand this ___ First ___ day of ___ October ___ , 19 ___ 87 .

_____ _Abraham Lee Light_ _____
(Testator signature)

This codicil to the LAST WILL AND TESTAMENT of _____ Abraham Lee Light .

was signed and declared to be his/~~her~~ codicil to his/~~her~~ LAST WILL AND TESTAMENT in our presence

at his/~~her~~ request and in his/~~her~~ presence and the presence of each other as witnesses on this_____

_____ First _____ day of ___ October ___ , 19 ___ 87 .

Arnold Raymond Firestone   116 Maple Dr., Salem Va.
(Witness signature)   *(Address)*

Robert James Townsend   604 West Main St. Salem, Virginia
(Witness signature)   *(Address)*

_____   _____
(Witness signature)   *(Address)*

Figure 8

CODICIL
SELF-PROVING CERTIFICATE

State of _____VIRGINIA_____

~~County~~/City of _____Salem_____

Before me, the undersigned authority, on this day personally appeared

_____Abraham Lee Light_____

Testator _____Arnold Raymond Firestone_____

Witness _____Robert James Townsend_____

Witness _____

Witness

known to me to be the Testator and Witnesses, respectively, whose names are signed to the attached or foregoing instrument and, all of these persons being by me first duly sworn, _____

_____Abraham Lee Light_____ , the testator, declared to me and to the witnesses in my presence that said instrument is a codicil to his/~~her~~ LAST WILL AND TESTAMENT dated _____June 26_____ , 19 _85_ , and that he/~~she~~ had willingly signed or directed another to sign the codicil for him/~~her~~, and executed it in the presence of said witnesses as his/~~her~~ free and voluntary act for the purposes therein expressed; that said witnesses stated before me that the foregoing codicil was executed and acknowledged by the testator as a codicil to his/~~her~~ LAST WILL AND TESTAMENT in the presence of said witnesses who, in his/~~her~~ presence and at his/~~her~~ request, and in the presence of each other, did subscribe their names thereto as attesting witnesses on the day of the date of said codicil, and that the testator, at the time of the execution of said codicil was of sound and disposing mind and memory.

_____Abraham Lee Light_____
(Testator signature)

_____Arnold Raymond Firestone_____
(Witness signature)

_____Robert James Townsend_____
(Witness signature)

Subscribed, sworn and acknowledged before me by

_____Abraham Lee Light_____ , the Testator,

and subscribed and sworn before me by _____Arnold Raymond Firestone_____
and Robert James Townsend

_____ , Witnesses,

this _____First_____ day of _____October_____ , 19 _87_ A.D.

Signed: _____M_ _Notary Public_

Notary Public

My Commission Expires: _____5-16-91_____

(Seal)

Figure 9

LAST WILL AND TESTAMENT

I, _____ Karen Louise Light _____ , resident
of the ___ County ___ of ___ Botetourt ___ in the State of ___ VIRGINIA ___ ,
being of sound mind, do make and declare the following to be my LAST WILL AND TESTAMENT
and expressly revoke all my prior wills and codicils and certify that I am not acting under undue
influence, duress or menace.

I. EXECUTOR

I appoint _____ Abraham Lee Light, my son _____ EXECUTOR
of this, my LAST WILL AND TESTAMENT. If this EXECUTOR is unable to serve for any reason,

then I appoint _____ Louise Beatrice Hale, my daughter, ___ EXECUTOR.
The EXECUTOR is empowered to carry out all provisions of this WILL.
The EXECUTOR shall have all statutory powers available under State law.
The EXECUTOR named shall not be required to post surety bond. I
direct that no outside appraisal be made of my estate, unless
required for estate tax purposes.
The EXECUTOR shall receive the sum of $35,000.00 as compensation.

II. BEQUESTS

I give my farmland in Botetourt County, Virginia, Parcels
104-1178, 104-1179 and 104-1180, to my three beloved children,
Abraham Lee Light, Naomi Karen White and Louise Beatrice Hale
in equal shares, per stirpes.

I give Brandy Run Farm in Botetourt County, Virginia, Parcels
101-4711, 101-4712, 101-4713 and 102-1008, to my four beloved
grandchildren, Carroll Abraham Light, II, Karen Beth Cotswold,
Charles James Hale and Dawn Lee Hale, in equal shares, per
stirpes.

I give ownership of Patent US-4891086 (Expiration date April
20, 2011) and all royalty rights thereto, to my sister-in-law,
Mary Alice Light.

I give my Steinway baby grand piano to my niece, Charlene Ruth
Brown, per stirpes.

I give my collection of first edition books and the walnut
bookcase housing them, which is located in the study at Brandy
Run Farm, to my niece, Susan Elizabeth Reynolds, per stirpes.

Figure 10

I give my oil painting, "Mountain Morning", painted by C. F. Bransky, to my good friend, Miriam Rogers Steele.

I give the sum of five thousand dollars ($5,000.00) to Hollins College, Hollins, Virginia for the general scholarship fund.

I give the sum of two thousand five hundred dollars ($2,500.00) to the Roanoke Chapter of the American Red Cross, 312 Church Avenue, Roanoke, Virginia for the general purposes of the organization.

I give my dear son, Abraham Lee Light, all my livestock and farm equipment located at Brandy Run Farm. I give my son, Abraham Lee Light, my 1960 Ford Convertible, Serial Number 06059581CJ and all my shares (100) of C.A.L., Ltd. stock.

I give my dear daughter, Louise Beatrice Hale, my 1984 Mercedes Benz 300 SD Sedan, Serial Number 1QR6785234B.

I give my dear daughter, Naomi Karen White, my LKG monogrammed silverware and all sterling silver serving pieces.

I give all my shares of AT&T, Pacific Gas & Light and IBM stock and all my personal and household personal property, excepting cash accounts, to my beloved daughters, Naomi Karen White and Louise Beatrice Hale in equal shares, per stirpes.

All cash accounts and the entire residue of my estate, I give to my beloved son, Abraham Lee Light, and direct that my Executor take further action regarding the settling of my estate in accord with my Letter of Instructions, dated March 1, 1985, attached to this document as we discussed.

To the members of my family, I wish to state my love for and pride in them all and express my desire that my great-grandchildren be told the background of their family and roots. With best wishes and hope for the future, I conclude this, my Last Will and Testament, at this point.

Figure 11

WILL
SELF-PROVING CERTIFICATE

State of ___VIRGINIA___

County/City of ___Botetourt___

Before me, the undersigned authority, on this day personally appeared

Testator ___Karen Louise Light___

___Phillip Roy Jamison___

Witness ___Emily Jane Jamison___

Witness _____

Witness _____

known to me to be the Testator and Witnesses, respectively, whose names are signed to the attached or foregoing instrument and, all of these persons being by me first duly sworn, _____

___Karen Louise Light___ , the testator, declared to me and to the witnesses in my presence that said instrument is his/her LAST WILL AND TESTAMENT and that he/she had willingly signed or directed another to sign the same for him/her, and executed it in the presence of said witnesses as his/her free and voluntary act for the purposes therein expressed; that said witnesses stated before me that the foregoing will was executed and acknowledged by the testator as his/her LAST WILL AND TESTAMENT in the presence of said witnesses who, in his/her presence and at his/her request, and in the presence of each other, did subscribe their names thereto as attesting witnesses on the day of the date of said will, and that the testator, at the time of the execution of said will was over the age of eighteen years and of sound and disposing mind and memory.

Karen Louise Light
___(Testator signature)___

Phillip Roy Jamison
___(Witness signature)___

Emily Jane Jamison
___(Witness signature)___

Subscribed, sworn and acknowledged before me by

___Karen Louise Light___ , the Testator,

and subscribed and sworn before me by ___Phillip Roy Jamison___

___and Emily Jane Jamison___

_____ , Witnesses,

this ___twelth___ day of ___March___ , 19 _85_ A.D.

Signed: *Ms. Palace Public*
___Notary Public___

My Commission Expires: ___3-31-87___

(Seal)

Figure 12

70

LETTER OF INSTRUCTIONS

March 1, 1985

To my Executor,

My husband Carroll and I discussed passing on the family farm many times before he died. The distribution of shares of ownership is set out in the will. I direct that the balance of cash accounts, after deductions of cash bequests and the agreed upon Executor's fee, be applied to estate taxes due. I direct that the commercial building, Lot 7, Blocks 131-135 in the City of Salem be sold and the proceeds be applied to estate taxes due. In the event that insufficient funds to pay all estate taxes will remain after my specific bequests have been made, I direct that my Executor arrange a loan for the balance needed, to be secured by the parcels of farmland 104-1178, 104-1179, 104-1180 located in Botetourt County, Virginia, prior to final transfer of encumbered title interests. I further direct my Executor to continue current farm lease payments to all owners of the farmland and Brandy Run Farm according to their share of ownership as long as the Brandy Run dairy farm and orchard is under family management. The lease payment income should offset most of the estate tax loan payment. I direct that this plan be followed by my children as I recognize that it will cause the least financial impact and that they all are of more than adequate means to carry it out.

I direct that my Executor transfer the patent rights to Carroll's fiber-optic switching control device to his sister, Mary Alice Light, and to close C.A.L., Ltd., the private corporation administering the royalty rights. I recognize that, if Mary Alice Light dies before me, the bequest will be adeemed, and revert to Abraham Lee Light. In that case, the instruction to close C.A.L.,Ltd. does not apply.

If in the division of my personal and household goods, my daughters should disagree, the matter is to be resolved by a flip of a coin, supervised by the Executor.

With love,

Karen Louise Light
Karen Louise Light

March 1, 1985

Figure 13

Looking Ahead

Because Abraham and his mother had discussed her wishes frequently and he was thoroughly familiar with the family's financial situation, he was able to settle her estate without encountering any unforeseen difficulties. Drawing on his experience as Executor, Abraham talked to his son, Carroll, and Carroll's wife, Jo Anne, about the importance of their wills and suggested how his grandchildren's interests might be protected. (See Figures 14 through 16.) He now understood how family wealth was built and was grateful for the foresight of his parents and grandparents. His family had been through a wide range of experiences, and the future was bright. Abraham completed his family history notes and gave Susan the names and dates to fill in on copies of the family tree that would become Christmas gifts for all of Carroll and Karen's descendants.

LAST WILL AND TESTAMENT

I, _____ Carroll Abraham Light, II _____ , resident
of the __City__ of _____ Salem _____ in the State of ____VIRGINIA____ ,
being of sound mind, do make and declare the following to be my LAST WILL AND TESTAMENT
and expressly revoke all my prior wills and codicils and certify that I am not acting under undue
influence, duress or menace.

I. EXECUTOR

I appoint _____ Jo Anne Stone Light, my wife, _____ EXECUTOR
of this my LAST WILL AND TESTAMENT. If this EXECUTOR is unable to serve for any reason,
then I appoint _____ Abraham Lee Light, my father _____ EXECUTOR.
The EXECUTOR is empowered to carry out all provisions of this WILL.
The EXECUTOR shall have all statutory powers available under State law.
The EXECUTOR named shall not be required to post surety bond. I direct that no outside appraisal
be made of my estate, unless required for estate tax purposes.

II. BEQUESTS

I give my entire estate to my beloved wife, Jo Anne
Stone Light, with the exception of my share of ownership of
Brandy Run Farm (Parcels 101-4711, 101-4712, 101-4713, 102-
1008) located in Botetourt County, Virginia, which I give to
my dear daughter, Linda Lee Light, and my dear son, Paul
Abraham Light, in equal shares.

If my wife, Jo Anne Stone Light, does not survive me by
more than 180 days, then I give my entire estate to my daughter,
Linda Lee Light, and my son, Paul Abraham Light, in equal
shares and appoint Abraham Lee Light, my father, as guardian
of my children until they attain their majority.

This ends my Last Will and Testament.

Figure 14

LAST WILL AND TESTAMENT

I, _____Jo Anne Stone Light_____ , resident

of the ___City___ of ___Salem_____ in the State of ___VIRGINIA___ ,

being of sound mind, do make and declare the following to be my LAST WILL AND TESTAMENT and expressly revoke all my prior wills and codicils and certify that I am not acting under undue influence, duress or menace.

I. EXECUTOR

I appoint ___Carroll Abraham Light, II, my husband___ EXECUTOR of this my LAST WILL AND TESTAMENT. If this EXECUTOR is unable to serve for any reason,

then I appoint ___Abraham Lee Light, my father-in-law,___ EXECUTOR.

The EXECUTOR is empowered to carry out all provisions of this WILL.

The EXECUTOR shall have all statutory powers available under State law.

The EXECUTOR named shall not be required to post surety bond. I direct that no outside appraisal be made of my estate, unless required for estate tax purposes.

II. BEQUESTS

I give my entire estate to my beloved husband, Carroll Abraham Light, II. If my husband, Carroll Abraham Light, II, dies before me, then I give my entire estate to my dear daughter, Linda Lee Light and my dear son, Paul Abraham Light, in equal shares and appoint Abraham Lee Light, my father-in-law, as guardian of my children until they attain their majority.

This ends my Last Will and Testament.

Figure 15

WILL
SELF-PROVING CERTIFICATE

State of ___VIRGINIA___

County/City of ___Salem___

Before me, the undersigned authority, on this day personally appeared

Jo Anne Stone Light

Testator   Ralph Peter Stanley

Witness   Martha Virginia Stanley

Witness

Witness

known to me to be the Testator and Witnesses, respectively, whose names are signed to the attached or foregoing instrument and, all of these persons being by me first duly sworn, ___Jo Anne Stone Light___, the testator, declared to me and to the witnesses in my presence that said instrument is ~~his~~/her LAST WILL AND TESTAMENT and that ~~he~~/she had willingly signed or directed another to sign the same for ~~him~~/her, and executed it in the presence of said witnesses as ~~his~~/her free and voluntary act for the purposes therein expressed; that said witnesses stated before me that the foregoing will was executed and acknowledged by the testator as ~~his~~/her LAST WILL AND TESTAMENT in the presence of said witnesses who, in ~~his~~/her presence and at ~~his~~/her request, and in the presence of each other, did subscribe their names thereto as attesting witnesses on the day of the date of said will, and that the testator, at the time of the execution of said will was over the age of eighteen years and of sound and disposing mind and memory.

Jo Anne Stone Light
(Testator signature)

Ralph Peter Stanley
(Witness signature)

Martha Virginia Stanley
(Witness signature)

Subscribed, sworn and acknowledged before me by

Jo Anne Stone Light , the Testator,

and subscribed and sworn before me by___Ralph Peter Stanley___

and Martha Virginia Stanley

_____ , Witnesses,

this ___seventeenth___ day of ___February___ , 19 _89_ A.D.

Signed: _M. Notary Public_
Notary Public

My Commission Expires: ___5-16-91___

(Seal)

Figure 16

75

CHAPTER 6

Executor's Guide

Your Executor is responsible for administering your estate and carrying out the terms of your will. The Executor will work closely with your family and beneficiaries during the probate process and become familiar with financial and personal details of your estate. Naming your spouse, major beneficiary, a relative, or a friend as Executor can save expense to the estate and help maintain privacy. The duties of the Executor are not difficult and normally require only routine recordkeeping and accounting ability. Your chosen Executor can employ professional assistance for specific probate tasks if needed. Careful and efficient administration by the Executor conserves your estate for your beneficiaries.

The duties of the Executor, though not complicated, require care, time, and attention to detail. Compensating the person you've chosen to settle your estate is usually unnecessary if you've named your spouse or other major beneficiary as Executor. If you name someone other than a primary beneficiary to settle your estate, you should discuss compensation and be sure that the named person consents to serve. Your Executor should be a responsible, trustworthy person who has concern for your family, beneficiaries, and estate. If no one close to you is able to act as your Executor, you should consider your options carefully. Most trust officers of financial institutions, attorneys, and other professionals offer Executor services on a fee basis. Before naming a professional Executor, discuss your estate plan, and agree to a fee schedule in advance.

Appointing an Executor

The Executor of an estate is nominated in the will of the Testator and, upon approval, appointed by the court of probate. "Letters Testamentary" are issued to the Executor as official proof of appointment. After formal appointment, the Executor must fulfill the duties prescribed by law and, to the extent possible, carry out the terms of the will. The duties and powers of the Executor are defined by state statute unless limited or expanded in the will. The Executor's role involves acting as the agent of the Testator to pay debts, expenses, and taxes the estate is liable for and to collect any debts, fees, or property due the estate. After debts, expenses, and taxes have been paid, the remaining property is given to the beneficiaries according to the terms of the will. With court approval, after all estate property has been distributed and accounted for, the estate is closed. Settling an estate is usually not difficult or costly, although patience and careful attention to detail are necessary. If certain tasks require skills and expertise beyond the capabilities of the Executor, he or she may obtain professional assistance. Saving expenses to the estate, which conserves assets for the beneficiaries, is a primary concern of the Executor.

The Appointment of an Administrator

Much of the information presented here about Executors applies also to those who petition the court to act as Administrator of an intestate estate. The Administrator and Executor perform similar functions in settling an estate, the primary difference being that the Executor distributes the estate according to the Testator's will, whereas the Administrator must distribute the estate according to state intestate succession law.

A member of the family of a person who dies intestate usually seeks appointment, although others with an interest in the estate may also apply. If no applicants are accepted by the court, or no one applies, the court appoints an Administrator, usually a local attorney. The Administrator is entitled, by law, to reasonable compensation, usually totaling 3–5 percent of the appraised value of the estate.

An intestate estate is administered according to state statutes, usually with close court supervision. The Administrator must post a surety bond, obtainable through a local bonding agent or company, to protect the assets of the estate.

Conserving and Collecting Assets

The estate of the Testator consists of all the real and personal property owned at the time of death. The duty of the Executor is to collect and conserve that property and, after all estate expenses have been paid, to distribute the remainder according to the terms of the will. Upon appointment, the Executor should promptly identify and secure all estate assets.

An inventory of the estate of the Testator will be needed during the probate process. It is the Executor's duty to exercise reasonable diligence in locating all estate assets. If the Executor is the spouse or primary beneficiary of the Testator, the type, location, and value of all assets are usually known. If the Executor is unfamiliar with the estate, a complete search for all real and personal assets will be necessary. Inquiries of relatives and friends, along with careful review of the records of the Testator, should locate most assets. A thorough search of records and receipts can reveal bank deposits, rental storage units, and other assets of the Testator. Any professional or family advisers may also be useful sources of information and assistance. After all estate assets are located and secured, the Executor should list, with adequate detail, the type of asset, location, and value. The completed inventory provides the basis for valuing the estate for state and federal estate tax purposes. Careful recordkeeping simplifies the tasks of accounting and tax filing.

As estate assets are collected, they must be conserved and protected. A separate bank account, with its own Federal Employer Identification Number (FEIN), should be opened in the name of the estate as soon as practicable. Any monies, proceeds from liquidated assets, or benefits due the Testator and estate are recorded and deposited in the estate account, and legitimate estate expenses are paid from that account. Do not neglect to file for Social Security death benefits and, if the decedent is eligible to receive them, Veterans Administration, Civil Service, and/or Railroad Retirement death benefits. If substantial cash assets are available, an interest-bearing account should be considered. Interest earned by the estate may be subject to federal and state income taxes. A separate account, with accurate and detailed records, is also useful in completing any tax returns for the estate.

Types of Administration and Accounting

The Executor must carry out the duties of administering the estate according to state requirements. Most states have both supervised and unsupervised administration of an estate, with the probate court determining the type of administration available to the Executor. The court, when deciding the type of administration, considers the nature and extent of the estate, its value, and the skills and abilities of the Executor. Fully supervised administration requires the Executor to seek court approval for almost all actions taken in the probate process. A complete inventory of estate assets, valued by court-approved appraisers, and a full audit of accounts may be required before debts are paid or any property is distributed to beneficiaries.

Unsupervised administration allows the Executor to perform many, if not all, probate tasks without prior court approval. The time and effort required of the Executor is minimized when this type of administration is used. The probate court determines the type of administration available to the Executor. Texas requires the use of the term independent Executor in the will for unsupervised administration.

Debts and Creditors

Creditors' claims against the estate, funeral expenses, and bills owed by the Testator must be examined for validity, reasonableness, and accuracy by the Executor. Under unsupervised administration, payment of many claims may be made by the Executor without specific court approval. In some states, the claims must be filed directly to the court and, upon approval, paid by the Executor. Each claim should be listed and the basis of the claim, the amount, the date due, and the name and address of the claimant noted. Monthly billing statements from credit card companies, retail stores, or others are usually valid claims of this type. Any time or demand notes due a bank or other financial institution, documented loans from individuals, and auto loans are included as well. Rent or lease payments owed by the Testator must be paid, and the Executor should notify rental agents/lessors immediately if property is vacated.

The Testator's creditors must be informed, by letter or public notice, of the opening of the estate and given the opportunity to present legitimate claims. In a few states, creditors must be contacted by letter or notice in the mail. The Executor must conduct a search for evidence of debt and notify the creditors within a time specified by the court. Public notice is a more common practice, and the process required to notify creditors is similar in most states. A notice is published in local newspapers informing anyone having a claim against the estate of the Testator's death and the opening of the estate for probate. The creditors are given a specific number of days to file their claim and any related documents. The exact requirements for this notice and the number of times it must be published can be obtained from the court of probate. If a creditor fails to file a claim in the period of time required by law, there is no legal obligation to pay the debt. In such a case, payment may be made at the discretion of the Executor/Administrator. If the assets of the Testator are insufficient to pay all the debts owed, they must be paid in an order determined by state law. Preferred claims are defined by state laws and must be paid before all others. These claims usually include funeral expenses, estate administration expenses, fees, and outstanding taxes due. It is important to obtain a receipt for every claim paid from the estate.

The remaining debts of the Testator are usually prorated and paid to the extent possible. If there is any question regarding a creditor's claim, the court should rule on its validity.

Personal property of the Testator may be encumbered by a debt or collateral situation. Release of such property may require the Executor to pay the balance outstanding from the estate assets. Repair bills for an automobile and redemption of pawned jewelry are typical examples. Rents on storage units or garages that are in arrears must be paid to secure the contents. Tools, lawn equipment, autos, boats, or other property lent to friends and any art or collections on loan for display should be secured as soon as practicable.

Real Property

Real estate and real property interests are the major assets of many estates. Real property owned by the Testator entirely and given to a specific beneficiary in the will must be maintained and insured to protect its value until title passes to the beneficiary. In the case of unimproved land, little if any maintenance is required, and insurance, with the possible exception of liability, is usually unnecessary. A house, building, or other structure must be protected with adequate insurance and should be maintained and secured. Payment of utilities and taxes must be made when due, as well as any homeowner or property association fees, regular maintenance charges, or other legitimate expenses. A vacant, neglected structure is a likely target for thieves and vandals and should be properly secured and maintained to prevent deterioration.

Ownership interests in real property may include partial interests in rental property, commercial buildings, or vacation property. In some states, "interval-ownership" (time-share) rights are also considered as real property and may be disposed of in a will. The Executor should obtain the originals or copies of all deeds or other title evidence to determine the ownership interest of the Testator.

The Testator may also own real estate as a joint tenant, tenant by the entirety, or tenant in common. Upon the death of a joint tenant with right of survivorship, or a tenant by the entirety, the property transfers to the surviving spouse or joint tenant, with no action required of the Executor. Though this property is not a part of the probate estate, the Executor must list the value of property transferred in this manner as part of the Testator's taxable estate. Property held as a tenant in common is owned individually and disposed of in the will. The Executor must list the interest held by the Testator as a tenant in common as an asset of the estate and distribute it under the terms of the will.

Liabilities against real property must be considered by the Executor in determining the true value of the property for tax purposes. Liabilities against real estate may include mortgages, home equity credit lines, reverse mortgages, life estates, and any taxes due against the property. Mortgage payments are usually continued by the Executor to allow the beneficiary flexibility in deciding whether to keep the existing mortgage, secure a new one, or sell the property. Other liabilities may have to be paid by the estate or beneficiary before the property can be transferred. Real estate owned by the Testator that is not in the state of residence requires the appointment of an ancillary representative who is a resident of the state in which the property is located. This person is responsible for the actual administration of the property and makes sure that appropriate state taxes are paid. The Executor must list out-of-state property when filing federal estate tax forms and include the value when determining if the estate exceeds the $600,000 exemption limit.

The Executor may, upon direction of the Testator and approval by the court, sell real property and distribute the proceeds as directed in the will. State laws differ in the authority given an Executor to dispose of real property. In some states, the Executor must have the approval of the court and beneficiaries before real estate is sold, while others allow the Executor to sell with few restrictions. If the Testator contracted to sell property prior to death, the Executor is usually required to complete the contract on the Testator's behalf and to account for the proceeds. It is always advisable to check with the court of probate before offering to sell real estate.

The value of real property owned by the Testator has a significant impact on the amount of federal and state taxes the estate will be liable for. In some situations, the Executor may be required to obtain a professional appraisal of the real assets for tax purposes. The Executor should carefully record and list the value of all property of the Testator, including nonprobate assets. Transactions regarding real property should be approved by the court of probate and the beneficiaries of the Testator.

Business Interests

Business interests of the Testator are usually transferred by a buy–sell agreement, stock transfer, or some other arrangement set out in advance. Because of potential personal liability, the Executor must exercise extreme care if business interests are included in the will of the Testator. The Executor, under most state laws, cannot continue business operations unless specifically authorized to do so in the will of the Testator. If no authorization is given, most states require the Executor to conserve the business for only as long as required to liquidate it. Under these circumstances, any continuance of the business must be done with court approval. If specific authorization is given to continue the business, the Executor is responsible for due care and operation of the business in a reasonable manner. Operation of a business is usually time-consuming and, in many situations, exposes the Executor to personal liability. Before taking any action regarding the Testator's business interests, the Executor should seek approval of the court and beneficiaries.

Distribution/Accounting

After assembling and securing the Testator's property, paying all debts, expenses, and taxes, the estate may be distributed. If the estate is properly disposed of by the Testator's will and is adequate to fulfill all bequests, this task can be simple. The Executor distributes the bequests and obtains receipts from the beneficiaries. Many states allow estates to be distributed without formal accounting when the beneficiaries are in agreement. Most courts also allow small estates, typically $10,000 or less, to be settled without formal accounting. Informal distribution is a simple procedure that avoids the additional expense and time required by a formal accounting.

If a formal accounting is called for, the Executor must follow state and local laws. The estate must be audited and all interested parties notified of the date and place of filing of the account. At the time of the audit, creditors, beneficiaries, or others with objections may be heard by the court. If the court approves of the audited account, a schedule of distribution is prepared, and the property is given to the designated beneficiary(ies). The Executor must have receipts from all beneficiaries before being released from his or her duties.

Taxes

The Executor is responsible for filing all federal and state tax forms on behalf of the Testator and estate. Care must be taken to determine the tax liability and appropriate filing dates. Federal tax liabilities may include income taxes owed by the Testator and, if any income is earned, by the estate as well. Federal estate tax is due if the total amount of the taxable estate exceeds $600,000.

The taxable estate of the Testator includes the probate assets and other taxable assets. Taxable gifts made after 1976, joint property and tenant-by-the-entirety interests, and the value of buy-sell agreements are included in the taxable estate. Life insurance proceeds may also be included in the taxable estate. The Executor should have accurate records of the value of the Testator's property, including the nonprobate assets, to determine if the estate is liable for federal estate tax.

State taxes can include income taxes, as well as other taxes related to the transfer of the estate. The state department of taxation and the court of probate can assist the Executor in determining current state estate tax requirements.

Executor Resources

Many resources are available to the Executor throughout the probate process. The best assistance is provided by the Testator who, if thorough, has left a current will along with complete records and instructions. An Executor should be as informed and aware of the Testator's estate plan as possible, preferably through prior discussion. The location of original documents, especially the will, records, and deeds needed to settle the estate, must be known to the Executor. A current will and adequate direction by the Testator can simplify the Executor's task immensely.

Accountants, appraisers, attorneys, and other professionals may be employed by the Executor in the probate process. Reasonable fees for professional assistance may be paid with estate assets in almost all situations. The Executor may often save expenses to the estate by employing professionals on an hourly basis while personally performing most routine probate tasks.

Personnel of the local court of probate, as public employees, are valuable resources that can provide the Executor basic information and other assistance. Developing a good working relationship with court personnel can often be of great value to the Executor during the probate process.

The position of Executor involves a close relationship with the family and friends of the Testator. The support and understanding of those close to the Testator can be especially helpful in the probate process. At the same time, personal concern and sensitivity on the part of the Executor can be a great comfort to those who have experienced a loss.

Executor's Checklist

The checklist on pages 86–89 is intended to provide general guidance for an Executor or Administrator of an estate. Not every task will be necessary for every estate; however, the entire checklist should be reviewed to make sure that nothing is overlooked. You may wish to retain a professional to assist you if the estate is complicated and requires extensive administration. An Executor works with the clerk of the local court throughout the probate process and should direct specific questions to that person, because requirements change over time.

To act efficiently on behalf of the Testator, it is important to have full understanding and knowledge of his or her estate plan. As soon as possible after you have agreed to act as Executor, discuss with the Testator the will, beneficiaries, and any instructions regarding the estate. The addresses and phone numbers of beneficiaries and the location of assets, property, and other estate components should be noted. Any professional advisers to the

Testator for legal, accounting, insurance, tax, or investment services should also be identified. The more information the Executor has about the estate, the easier estate administration becomes. Encourage the Testator to list *all* the relevant information needed to settle the estate. If business interests or other matters requiring continuing administration are involved, be sure to have a clear understanding of the details.

Executor's Checklist

_____   Locate the original of the last will of the Testator and any related documents.

_____   Obtain several copies of the death certificate.

NOTE: If no will is found, petition the court to administer the estate.

_____   Submit documents to the clerk of the court having jurisdiction over probate in the locality where the Testator was a legal resident to start the probate process. Refer to the State Summary for the name of the court having jurisdiction over probate.

Court: _____

Address: _____

_____

Clerk: _____

Phone: (   ) _____

_____   Have court confirm appointment as Executor.

NOTE: If nonresident, make arrangement for resident personal representative, if required.

_____   Post surety bond, if required.

_____   Obtain letters of administration from court.

_____   Elect unsupervised or small estate status, if available.

_____   Request that court confirm appointment of guardian(s).

_____   Arrange for ancillary probate administration of property located in other states.

_____   Consider the surviving spouse's right of election.

_____   Notify all interested persons of the opening of the probate process.

Executor's Checklist (*continued*)

_____ Arrange for notice of creditors as required in state.

_____ Apply for Federal Employer Identification Number (FEIN) for estate.

_____ Open bank account(s) for estate.

_____ Contact Testator's employer for unpaid salary and benefits, such as life insurance.

_____ File claims for life insurance.

_____ File for any Social Security, Civil Service, Veterans Administration, or other death and pension benefits.

_____ Identify and expedite transfer of property not subject to probate (trusts, jointly held property).

_____ Provide funds for allowable living expenses to surviving spouse and dependents with approval of local court.

_____ Notify utilities, post office, creditors, etc., of Testator's death and transfer accounts to survivors or estate as appropriate.

_____ Open and inventory all safe deposit boxes; transfer contents of estate safe deposit box, if necessary.

NOTE: Some states require that a representative of the state be present at the opening of the decedent's safe deposit box.

_____ Review financial records and recent tax returns of Testator.

_____ Prepare list of all beneficiaries, including Social Security numbers.

_____ Prepare preliminary estimate of value of estate.

_____ Appraise estate assets for a "date of death" valuation.

_____ Engage professional appraisers, if required by court or for tax purposes.

_____ Check with court for any claims filed against estate.

(*continued*)

Executor's Checklist (*continued*)

_____ Inspect all real estate and review mortgages, leases, property insurance policies, etc.

_____ Arrange for management of real property located in other states.

_____ Make arrangements for such special concerns as business interests and ongoing farming operations.

_____ Collect all property belonging, or owed, to the estate.

_____ Prepare and file Testator's personal federal and state income tax returns for portion of last year of life.

NOTE: Qualified widow/widower status is available if dependent children live with surviving spouse.

_____ Determine cash needs of estate.

_____ Arrange sale of estate property, if required.

_____ Pay all valid claims, bills, and expenses, with court approval if required.

_____ Prepare complete detailed inventory and appraisal of entire estate and file it with the court, with copies to major beneficiaries.

_____ Prepare and file federal and state estate income tax returns for period of administration.

_____ File federal and state estate tax returns, if applicable.

NOTE: A certified copy of the will must be attached to estate tax returns.

_____ Obtain court authorization to pay professional fees, if applicable.

_____ Distribute all assets as set out in will.

_____ Prepare final account of estate assets and distribution with receipts, and file it with the court.

Executor's Checklist (*continued*)

_____   Close estate, and obtain documents from court indicating completion of Executor's duties.

_____   Retain copies of all records in a personal file for at least three years.

CHAPTER 7

Taxes

Background

Because of the $600,000 federal estate tax exemption and the unlimited marital deduction, most estates face no federal estate tax liability at this time. When preparing an estate plan, you should note the value of real estate and other assets that may be included in your taxable estate. Appreciation, especially in real property values, can significantly affect your taxable estate. If your estate is approaching the exemption level, you should consider additional estate planning methods that can lower tax liabilities. Married couples should calculate the combined value of their taxable estates when making estate planning decisions. Federal estate taxes, marital deductions, taxable estate components, and other related topics are discussed in this chapter. State taxes, including state estate tax, income tax, credit estate tax, and inheritance taxes are also discussed and explained.

Death and taxes have been linked since Caesar Augustus created the first estate tax, set at 5 percent, to maintain the armies of the Roman Empire. The Roman system was in effect in Britain until 1066, when the Norman invasion introduced principles of French feudal law.

In 1540, the Statute of Wills was made a part of English Common Law and established methods of distribution of real property as well as different intestate succession criteria. Because this system was based on real property, which was of primary importance in the agrarian-based society, the marital rights of the dower and curtesy and the principle of homestead were established. English Common Law was the starting point of most of the estate laws of the United States.

French legal influence is evident in the state laws of Louisiana, a community-property state, where a parent may not completely disinherit a child. Most of the other community-property states were influenced by Spanish legal practice, which was similar to that of the French.

Another factor affecting the estate laws was the period in which they were enacted and subsequently revised, which depends to some extent on the time of statehood. Laws enacted in different centuries and decades naturally differ, as do laws that result from longer or shorter periods of testing, experience, and revision. With all these different components and legal traditions, it is not surprising that requirements relating to wills, estates, probate, intestate succession, and estate and inheritance taxes have varied greatly from state to state. Since about 1900, however, the federal taxation system and promotion of various model legistative acts dealing with such things as simultaneous death, probate, and living wills have worked to produce more uniformity in state laws.

Recently, the trend toward greater uniformity has accelerated. Extensive revision of federal estate and gift taxation law was initiated in 1981 and, in 1987, new provisions were fully phased in. One result is that all states (except Nevada, which imposes no death taxes at all) based their estate tax on the federal schedule of credit for state death taxes. Many states impose additional estate, gift, generation-skip transfer, and inheritance taxes on property passing through the probate process.

Your Estate

Your estate consists of everything you own or retain a controlling interest in and includes any amounts owed to you (unless uncollectible). Estate components may include:

- Real property
- Tangible personal property
- Intangible personal property
- Intellectual property
- Life insurance proceeds
- Annuities/pensions (with survivor payments)
- Custodial accounts
- Debts and sums receivable
- Business ownership

- Inheritances paid to your estate
- Taxable gifts (after 1976)

The total of your estate is known as your gross estate. Your gross estate is reduced by your outstanding liabilities and certain other expenses to calculate your taxable estate. Amounts deductible from the gross estate when the taxable estate is figured are:

- Administration and funeral expenses
- Claims against the estate
- Any outstanding obligation to which the property is subject
- Casualty and theft losses
- Marital deductions
- Charitable deductions

Certain items included in your gross estate, such as custodial accounts, do not pass under the terms of your will and hence are not included in your probate estate. As a result, the values of your gross estate, taxable estate, and probate estate are usually different.

Federal Taxes

INCOME TAX

Federal income tax will be due on income received by the Testator during the last year of life. Responsibility for filing the final income tax return falls on the Executor of the estate. The final income tax return is due on the former taxpayer's regular annual schedule. For calendar-year filers, the final return will be due April 15 of the year after death, or later if an extension of time to file is requested and obtained. It is advisable for the widow or widower to determine whether joint or separate filing status is more advantageous for a final return and to file accordingly.

Qualified widows and widowers (those who provide over half the living costs of a dependent child and do not remarry) may elect to use joint filing status for two years. A spouse who remarries during the same tax year as the death of a Testator may not file a final joint return with the deceased.

When your Executor takes charge of your affairs, a Federal Employer Identification Number (FEIN) is applied for. This number identifies the estate as a distinct entity. Income to the estate, such as interest, dividends, rents, and royalties, is subject to federal income tax if it exceeds $600 during any tax year prior to complete settlement of the estate. Your Executor is responsible for filing the estate income tax return.

Members of the U.S. Armed Forces who die while on active duty in a combat zone have their income tax liability abated (forgiven) for all tax years since beginning service in the combat zone. If income tax has been paid, a return may be claimed on behalf of the estate. This income tax abatement also applies to death resultant from wounds, disease, or injury incurred in a combat zone (after June 24, 1950). Estates of members of the U.S. Armed Forces officially listed as missing in action (MIA) are entitled to the same income tax abatement. Both military and civilian employees of the United States who die as a result of a terroristic or military action outside the United States (after November 17, 1978) are also eligible for income tax abatement from the time the fatal wound or injury was incurred. Special forms available from the Department of Defense or the Department of State must accompany the estate's request for income tax abatement.

ESTATE TAX

Federal estate tax is a tax on the *transfer* of property resultant from death. Currently, if the value of the gross estate at death is less than $600,000, the estate exemption threshold, no federal estate tax will be due. The taxable estate may be reduced below the $600,000 threshold if property passes to a surviving spouse. All property left to a surviving spouse may be deducted from the taxable estate utilizing *Schedule M, Bequests, Etc., to Surviving Spouse.* This marital deduction is unlimited as to amount and, if used, has the effect of deferring federal estate taxation until the death of the surviving spouse. If you are married and have a sizeable estate, you may wish to distribute up to the $600,000 threshold amount to others, with the balance to your spouse. This approach can reduce the total estate tax liability compared to that incurred if all property is given to the surviving spouse and the first $600,000 available exemption is not used. As of November 10, 1988, no marital deduction is available to a surviving spouse who is not a U.S. citizen. However, a marital deduction is allowed for property passing in a qualified domestic trust to a surviving alien spouse.

Life insurance proceeds paid to your estate or to your Executor are included in your gross taxable estate for federal estate tax purposes. Further, life insurance proceeds that are not payable to, or for the benefit of, your estate can be included in your federal gross taxable estate if you hold any of the incidents of ownership in the policy on the following list.

- Legal ownership of the policy
- The power to change beneficiaries
- The power to revoke an assignment
- The right to obtain a loan against the policy
- The right to surrender or cancel the policy

Rights that are not considered to be incidents of ownership include the right to receive dividends and the right to veto the sale of the policy by the trustee of an irrevocable trust funded by insurance. Careful review of your life insurance policies is necessary to determine federal estate tax implications.

If the total fair market value of the estate assets decreases in the six months after death, the alternate valuation method may also be used to reduce or eliminate federal estate tax liability. The alternate valuation method values property when sold, transferred, or distributed and all undistributed assets at their value six months after the date of death rather than on the actual date of death. The maximum amount by which an estate may be decreased using the alternate valuation method is limited to $750,000.

If a federal estate tax return (IRS Form 706) is required, your executor must file it within nine months after the actual date of death. Refer to Chapter 8 for a completed sample of IRS Form 706.

Owners of farms and closely held businesses, when the farm or business real property constitutes a substantial portion of the gross estate, should be aware that their Executors may also elect special-use valuation, basing value on return from use rather than fair market value. Additionally, longer installment payment options for federal estate tax due are available to owners of farms and closely held businesses, subject to various situation-specific requirements.

GIFT TAX

Federal gift tax is incurred when a "taxable gift" is made. Currently, a taxable gift is the value of any gift to a person in excess of $10,000 in the donor's tax year. Stated conversely, gifts of $10,000 or less are exempt from gift taxes. Previously, gift taxes and estate taxes were reported and collected separately and had different taxation rates. However, congressional action created a unification of these two taxes at a single rate. As a result, as of 1977, taxable gifts must be taken into account when calculating federal estate tax liability. The total amount of adjusted taxable gifts is subtracted from the $600,000 federal estate tax exemption level. If you have made substantial adjusted taxable gifts over the last twelve years, be aware of the lower threshold exemption level available to the estate. Note that qualified transfers, which are amounts paid to an educational organization as tuition or to a health-care institution for medical care on behalf of another, are not considered taxable gifts for tax calculation purposes.

In addition to the reduction of the $600,000 federal estate tax exemption by the amount of adjusted taxable gifts, be aware that generation-skipping transfers are included when figuring the total amount of the taxable estate subject to federal estate tax. Since the general policy regarding federal estate tax is to tax the transfer of property at the point of generational change (normally the death of the surviving spouse), gifts to grandchildren or others at least two generations removed from the Testator are included in the gross estate. If generation-skipping transfers have been included in your estate plan, it is advisable to review the terms and methods in light of current federal estate tax.

State Taxes

INCOME TAX

State income tax will be due on income received by the Testator during the last year of life in those states that impose income tax. Filing the state tax return on the former taxpayer's usual tax-year basis is the responsibility of the Executor. Income to the estate above the state's annual minimum will also be subject to a state income tax each tax year until the estate is settled and closed.

ESTATE TAX

All states except Nevada impose federal credit estate taxes. Additionally, seven states (Massachusetts, Mississippi, New York, Ohio, Oklahoma, Rhode Island, and South Carolina) impose estate taxes at state-determined rates on the estate after certain deductions. The federal credit estate tax amounts are shown on the following Federal (IRS) Credit for State Death Taxes schedule. The schedule applies to the taxable amount of the estate (currently the federal taxable estate, less $60,000). This method is known as federal credit estate taxation, and it starts with taxable estates in excess of $160,000 (after subtracting the $60,000 deduction).

Credit for State Death Taxes

A	B	C	D
Taxable Amount Equal to or Over	Taxable Amount Not Over	Credit on Amount in Column A	Rate of Credit on Excess Over Amount in Column A (%)
$ 100,000	$ 150,000	0	0.8
150,000	200,000	$ 400	1.6
200,000	300,000	1,200	2.4
300,000	500,000	3,600	3.2
500,000	700,000	10,000	4.0
700,000	900,000	18,000	4.8
900,000	1,100,000	27,600	5.6
1,100,000	1,600,000	38,800	6.4
1,600,000	2,100,000	70,800	7.2
2,100,000	2,600,000	106,800	8.0
2,600,000	3,100,000	146,800	8.8
3,600,000	4,100,000	238,800	10.4

(continued)

Credit for State Death Taxes (*continued*)

A Taxable Amount Equal to or Over	B Taxable Amount Not Over	C Credit on Amount in Column A	D Rate of Credit on Excess Over Amount in Column A (%)
4,100,000	5,100,000	290,800	11.2
5,100,000	6,100,000	402,800	12.0
6,100,000	7,100,000	522,800	12.8
7,100,000	8,100,000	650,800	13.6
8,100,000	9,100,000	786,800	14.4
9,100,000	10,100,000	930,800	15.2
10,100,000	—	1,082,800	16.0

INHERITANCE TAX

Inheritance tax is a tax imposed on *receipt* of property resultant from death. Inheritance tax is due from the person who receives the Testator's property and is usually withheld from the amount of the bequest prior to distribution. Inheritance tax rates vary from state to state and with the relationship of the beneficiary to the Testator. Twenty-two states currently impose an inheritance tax. Inheritance tax is separate from, and additional to, federal credit estate tax and state estate tax.

State inheritance and estate taxes are assessed on real property, personal property, and intangible personal property. State taxes apply to real property located within the state. Similarly, personal property located within a state is taxed by that state. If a person has residences in more than one state, taxing jurisdiction for intangible personal property such as stocks, bonds, and notes is the same as that of the primary residence or domicile. The primary residence is the one occupied for more than six months a year. Other jurisdiction factors include voter registration, issuance of a driver's license, and location of active checking and bank accounts. If you maintain residences in more than one state, it is important to establish your domicile clearly; otherwise, the states involved may all attempt to impose estate and inheritance taxes, thereby causing additional delay and expense in settling your estate.

GIFT TAX

Six states (Delaware, Louisiana, New York, North Carolina, Tennessee, and Wisconsin) also levy gift taxes. Generally, credit for gift taxes paid at the state level is handled in a similar manner as it is for federal gift taxes. Fifteen states (refer to the State Summary, Chapter 9) have followed the federal lead and have included generation-skipping transfers when calculating estate tax liability. These states have referenced the federal regulations regarding definitions and reporting of generation-skipping transfers.

Insufficient Assets

If your estate is not sufficient to pay all your debts, each state establishes the priority of claims against the estate. Generally, payment of expenses and debts is in the following order:

1. Court fees and costs
2. Funeral, burial, or cremation expenses
3. Estate administration costs, fees, and expenses (legal fees, personal representative compensation, and real estate brokerage commissions from sale of the estate's real property)
4. Spousal and family allowance
5. Taxes
6. Reasonable expenses for last illness (medical, hospital, nursing)
7. Last three months of rent in arrears
8. Last three months of wages, salaries, or commissions due to be paid
9. All other claims

Given insufficient funds remaining after priorities 1–8 (above) have been paid, all claims listed under priority 9 must be paid proportionally. If all these costs have been paid, bequests will be honored in the following sequence:

1. Specific and monetary bequests
2. A general (not source- or item-specific) bequest to the surviving spouse
3. General bequest to others
4. Residual bequest(s)

Clearly, if review of your estate reveals a potential shortfall, it is prudent to purchase life insurance in an amount sufficient to deal with the situation or to develop another contingency plan.

8

U.S. Estate Tax Return: Sample Form 706

Filing

A U.S. Estate Tax Return (IRS Form 706) must be filed if the total of the gross estate and adjusted taxable gifts made after 1976 exceeds $600,000. The U.S. Estate Tax Return must be filed within nine months of death, unless an Application for Extension of Time to File (IRS Form 4768) is filed within the nine-month period and granted by the Internal Revenue Service. Also, a copy of the death certificate and a certified copy of the will must be filed with the U.S. Estate Tax Return. Filing of the U.S. Estate Tax Return is the responsibility of the Executor of the estate; if there is more than one Executor, Co-Executors must all sign the return.

While a U.S. Estate Tax Return must be filed for all estates exceeding $600,000, the amount passing to a surviving spouse may be deducted on Schedule M. If this unlimited marital deduction reduces the gross taxable estate, including adjusted taxable gifts, to less than $600,000, no federal estate tax will be due. Use of the unlimited marital deduction has the effect of postponing federal estate taxation until the death of the surviving spouse.

Alternate Valuation

The sample U.S. Estate Tax Return that begins on page 103 is provided to illustrate a completed IRS Form 706 for an estate that cannot utilize the unlimited marital deduction because there is no surviving spouse. In this example, there are no trusts involved. Schedule P, Credit for Foreign Death Taxes; Schedule Q, Credit for Tax on Prior Transfers; and Schedule R, Generation-Skipping Transfer Tax, have been omitted as they do not apply to this sample estate. In this sample, the Executor has elected special-use valuation for the family farm and has chosen alternate valuation, that is, valuation six months after the actual date of death, rather than date-of-death valuation. Review of the sample shows how these elections reduced the taxable gross estate by $639,000, thereby reducing the total federal estate tax liability by approximately $320,000. Also included in this sample U.S. Estate Tax Return are two sample IRS 712 Life Insurance Statement forms. These forms, which are prepared by the life insurance companies holding policies on the decedent, must accompany Schedule D, Insurance on the Decedent's Life. You will note that while all life insurance policies must be reported, they may or may not be included in the gross estate, depending on whether the decedent had any incidents of ownership.

This sample shows the U.S. Estate Tax Return for Karen Louise Light, whose sample will was shown in Chapter 5. (All sample material is fictitious.)

Karen Louise Greene married Carroll A. Light in 1934. The couple moved to the greater Los Angeles area and had three children, Abraham L. Light, Naomi K. Light, and Louise B. Light. When Carroll's mother died in 1954, the Lights moved to the family farm, Brandy Run, in Botetourt County, Virginia. The Lights ran Brandy Run as a dairy farm and orchard and purchased additional adjoining proeprty. Abraham L. Light assisted his father in the successful dairy business until he took over complete management of the enterprise.

Carroll A. Light died in 1984, leaving the bulk of his estate to his wife, Karen. As previously agreed, Abraham then began to pay a lease fee to his mother for use of the acreage and improvements in the dairy operation. This arrangement provided her with a steady source of supplemental income. In 1988, Karen L. Light had made plans to fly to Los Angeles to meet two of her old friends. From there, the three were going on to Hawaii. She charged her plane tickets on her credit card, which carried automatic flight insurance. The plane, which took off from Washington, D.C. on June 14, 1988, crashed in Utah, and Karen died in Young Memorial Hospital three days later without regaining consciousness.

Because Karen Light had discussed her estate plans and concerns with Abraham, her chosen Executor, he was able to settle her estate confidently. Title to the original Brandy Run farm passed to her grandchildren, and the additional acreage passed to her children. Abraham carried on the dairy operation, and the land lease payments continued to provide income for the landowners. The renewed royalty payment rights from Carroll Light's switching devices were given to his sister, Mary, and the Light private corporation administering them was dissolved.

Special-Use Valuation

As Executor, Abraham L. Light elected special-use valuation for the working farm and chose alternate valuation after ascertaining that the value of Karen's stocks had fallen appreciably as of the alternate valuation date. Abraham paid out the Executor's fee he and his mother had agreed on. This was not only fair compensation, but it reduced the taxable gross estate. Nonetheless, the total of state and federal estate taxes amounted to over $750,000. This tax amount was paid from the cash accounts (Schedule C), the proceeds of the automatic flight insurance (Schedule D), and the sale of the commercial property (Schedule A), leaving a shortfall of approximately $210,000. This balance was satisfied by obtaining a loan against the three children's adjoining parcels, as suggested in Karen's letter of instructions. Clearly, careful thought and planning are required to minimize the amount of estate taxes. In this case, the taxes due could have been reduced further if Carroll A. Light had dispersed more of his estate (up to the untaxed maximum) to others than his wife or if trusts had been established by Karen for the grandchildren's interests.

NOTE: This sample uses the most recent IRS 706 forms available at press time. Most of the recent estate tax legislative changes have been incorporated into these forms. However, the previously scheduled decline in federal estate tax rates has been deferred until 1993. Consequently, it is always advisable to contact the Internal Revenue Service to obtain the most recent forms. The following IRS publications will also be of value in settling an estate:

IRS PUB-559 Tax Information for Survivors, Executors and Administrators

IRS PUB-448 Federal Estate & Gift Taxes

See the last page of this chapter for information on how to order IRS forms and publications.

Sample IRS Forms

Forms Omitted from Sample

Form **706**
(Rev. October 1988)
Department of the Treasury
Internal Revenue Service

United States Estate (and Generation-Skipping Transfer)
Tax Return
Estate of a citizen or resident of the United States (see separate instructions). To be
filed for decedents dying after October 22, 1986, and before January 1, 1990.
For Paperwork Reduction Act Notice, see page 1 of the instructions.

OMB No. 1545-0015
Expires 8-30-91

Part 1.—Decedent and Executor

1a Decedent's first name and middle initial (and maiden name, if any)	1b Decedent's last name	2 Decedent's social security no.
Karen L. Greene	Light	070 : 68 : 4921

3a Domicile at time of death	3b Year domicile established	4 Date of birth	5 Date of death
Botetourt County, Virginia	1954	3/15/12	6/17/88

6a Name of executor (see instructions)	6b Executor's address (number and street including apartment number or rural route; city, town, or post office; state; and ZIP code)
Abraham L. Light	
6c Executor's social security number (see instructions) 429 : 06 : 1762	236 Mountain View Drive Salem, VA 24153

7a Name and location of court where will was probated or estate administered	7b Case number
Botetourt County Circuit Court, Fincastle, Virginia 24090	88-71-0439

8 If decedent died testate, check here ▶ [X] and attach a certified copy of the will.   **9** If Form 4768 is attached, check here ▶ ☐

10 If Schedule R-1 is attached, check here ▶ ☐   *See page 2 for representative's authorization.*

Part 2.—Tax Computation

1	Total gross estate (from Part 5, Recapitulation, page 3, item 10)	1	2,417,820 -
2	Total allowable deductions (from Part 5, Recapitulation, page 3, item 25)	2	71,576 -
3	Taxable estate (subtract line 2 from line 1)	3	2,346,244 -
4	Adjusted taxable gifts (total taxable gifts (within the meaning of section 2503) made by the decedent after December 31, 1976, other than gifts that are includible in decedent's gross estate (section 2001(b)))	4	16,000 -
5	Add lines 3 and 4	5	2,362,244 -
6	Tentative tax on the amount on line 5 from Table A in the instructions	6	958,300 -

Note: *If decedent died before January 1, 1988, skip lines 7a-c and enter the amount from line 6 on line 8.*

7a	If line 5 exceeds $10,000,000, enter the lesser of line 5 or $21,040,000. If line 5 is $10,000,000 or less, skip lines 7a and 7b and enter zero on line 7c	7a		
b	Subtract $10,000,000 from line 7a	7b		
c	Enter 5% (.05) of line 7b		7c	-0-
8	Total tentative tax (add lines 6 and 7c)		8	958,300 -
9	Total gift tax payable with respect to gifts made by the decedent after December 31, 1976. Include gift taxes paid by the decedent's spouse for split gifts (section 2513) only if the decedent was the donor of these gifts and they are includible in the decedent's gross estate (see instructions)		9	3,000
10	Gross estate tax (subtract line 9 from line 8)		10	955,300 -
11	Unified credit against estate tax from Table B in the instructions	11 192,800 -		
12	Adjustment to unified credit. (This adjustment may not exceed $6,000. See instructions.)	12 -0-		
13	Allowable unified credit (subtract line 12 from line 11)		13	192,800 -
14	Subtract line 13 from line 10 (but do not enter less than zero)		14	762,500 -
15	Credit for state death taxes. Do not enter more than line 14. Compute credit by using amount on line 3 less $60,000. See Table C in the instructions and **attach credit evidence** (see instructions)		15	126,498 -
16	Subtract line 15 from line 14		16	636,002 -
17	Credit for Federal gift taxes on pre-1977 gifts (section 2012)(attach computation)	17 -0-		
18	Credit for foreign death taxes (from Schedule(s) P). (Attach Form(s) 706CE)	18 -0-		
19	Credit for tax on prior transfers (from Schedule Q)	19 -0-		
20	Total (add lines 17, 18, and 19)		20	-0-
21	Net estate tax (subtract line 20 from line 16)		21	636,002 -
22	Generation-skipping transfer taxes (from Schedule R, Part 2, line 12)		22	-0-
23	Section 4980A increased estate tax (attach Schedule S (Form 706)) (see instructions)		23	-0-
24	Total transfer taxes (add lines 21, 22, and 23)		24	636,002 -
25	Prior payments. Explain in an attached statement	25 -0-		
26	United States Treasury bonds redeemed in payment of estate tax	26 -0-		
27	Total (add lines 25 and 26)		27	-0-
28	Balance due (subtract line 27 from line 24)		28	636,002 -

Under penalties of perjury, I declare that I have examined this return, including accompanying schedules and statements, and to the best of my knowledge and belief, it is true, correct, and complete. Declaration of preparer other than the executor is based on all information of which preparer has any knowledge.

Signature(s) of executor(s) _Abraham Lee Light_   Date 3-15-89

Signature of preparer other than executor _____   Address (and ZIP code) _____   Date _____

103

Estate of: Karen L. Light

Part 3.—Elections by the Executor

Please check the "Yes" or "No" box for each question.	Yes	No
1 Do you elect alternate valuation?	X	
2 Do you elect special use valuation? . . . . If "Yes," you must complete and attach Schedule A–1	X	
3 Do you elect to pay the taxes in installments as described in section 6166? . . . . If "Yes," you must attach the additional information described in the instructions.		X
4 Do you elect to postpone the part of the taxes attributable to a reversionary or remainder interest as described in section 6163?		X
5 Do you elect to have part or all of the estate tax liability assumed by an Employee Stock Ownership Plan (ESOP) as described in section 2210? If "Yes," enter the amount of tax assumed by the ESOP here ▶$ _____ and attach the supplemental statements described in the instructions.		X

Part 4.—General Information Note: *Please attach the necessary supplemental documents.* **You must attach the death certificate.**

Authorization to receive confidential tax information under Regulations section 601.502(c)(3)(ii), to act as the estate's representative before the Internal Revenue Service, and to make written or oral presentations on behalf of the estate if return prepared by an attorney, accountant, or enrolled agent for the executor:

Name of representative (print or type)	State	Address (number and street, city, state, and ZIP code)

I declare that I am the attorney/accountant/enrolled agent (strike out the words that do not apply) for the executor and prepared this return for the executor. I am not under suspension or disbarment from practice before the Internal Revenue Service and am qualified to practice in the state shown above.

Signature		CAF Number	Date	Telephone Number

1 Death certificate number and issuing authority (attach a copy of the death certificate to this return).

0-088354   Young Memorial Hospital, Provo, Utah   84601

2 Decedent's business or occupation. If retired, check here ▶ ☒ and state decedent's former business or occupation.

Author

3 Marital status of the decedent at time of death:

☐ Married

☒ Widow or widower—Name, SSN and date of death of deceased spouse ▶ Carroll Abraham Light
021-76-8732,   12/19/84

☐ Single

☐ Legally separated

☐ Divorced—Date divorce decree became final ▶

4a Surviving spouse's name	4b Social security number	4c Amount received (see instructions)

5 Individuals (other than the surviving spouse), trusts, or other estates who receive benefits from the estate (do not include charitable beneficiaries shown in Schedule O) (see instructions). For Privacy Act Notice (applicable to individual beneficiaries only), see the Instructions for Form 1040.

Name of individual, trust or estate receiving $5,000 or more	Identifying number	Relationship to decedent	Amount (see instructions)
Abraham L. Light	429-06-1762	Son	$ 623,000.00
Naomi K. White	538-14-0227	Daughter	285,775.00
Louise B. Hale	601-23-4009	Daughter	285,775.00
Carroll A. Light, II	611-40-6311	Grandson	150,000.00
Karen B. Cotswold	612-59-0723	Granddaughter	150,000.00
Charles J. Hale	613-21-6897	Grandson	150,000.00
Dawn L. Hale	615-86-0820	Granddaughter	150,000.00
Mary L. Light	060-99-1234	Sister-in-Law	35,000.00
Miriam R. Steele	076-15-7642	Friend	7,200.00

All unascertainable beneficiaries and those who receive less than $5,000 . . . . ▶			6,000.00
Total			$1,842,750.00

(Continued on next page)   **Page 2**

Form 706 (Rev. 10-88)

Part 4.—General Information *(continued)*   Karen L. Light

Please check the "Yes" or "No" box for each question.

		Yes	No
6	Does the gross estate contain any section 2044 property (see instructions)?		X
7a	Have Federal gift tax returns ever been filed?	X	
	If "Yes," please attach copies of the returns, if available, and furnish the following information:		

7b Period(s) covered	7c Internal Revenue office(s) where filed		
1979, 1980	Memphis, TN 37501		

If you answer "Yes" to any of questions 8–16, you must attach additional information as described in the instructions.

		Yes	No
8a	Was there any insurance on the decedent's life that is not included on the return as part of the gross estate?	X	
b	Did the decedent own any insurance on the life of another that is not included in the gross estate?		X
9	Did the decedent at the time of death own any property as a joint tenant with right of survivorship in which (1) one or more of the other joint tenants was someone other than the decedent's spouse, and (2) less than the full value of the property is included on the return as part of the gross estate? If "Yes," you must complete and attach Schedule E		X
10	Did the decedent, at the time of death, own any interest in a partnership or unincorporated business or any stock in an inactive or closely held corporation?	X	
11a	Did the decedent make any transfer described in section 2035, 2036, 2037 or 2038 (see the instructions for Schedule G)? If "Yes," you must complete and attach Schedule G		X
b	If "Yes," was it a valuation freeze subject to section 2036(c)?		
12	Were there in existence at the time of the decedent's death:		
a	Any trusts created by the decedent during his or her lifetime?		X
b	Any trusts not created by the decedent under which the decedent possessed any power, beneficial interest, or trusteeship?		X
13	Did the decedent ever possess, exercise, or release any general power of appointment? If "Yes," you must complete and attach Schedule H.		X
14	Was the marital deduction computed under the transitional rule of Public Law 97-34, section 403(e)(3) (Economic Recovery Tax Act of 1981)?		X
	If "Yes," attach a separate computation of the marital deduction, enter the amount on item 18 of the Recapitulation, and note on item 18 "computation attached."		
15	Was the decedent, immediately before death, receiving an annuity described in the "General" paragraph of the instructions for Schedule I? If "Yes," you must complete and attach Schedule I.	X	
16	Did the decedent have a total "excess retirement accumulation" (as defined in section 4980A(d)) in qualified employer plan(s) and individual retirement plan(s)? If "Yes," you must attach Schedule S (Form 706) (see instructions)		X

Part 5.—Recapitulation

Item number	Gross estate	Alternate value	Value at date of death
1	Schedule A—Real Estate	1,065,000 –	1,070,000 –
2	Schedule B—Stocks and Bonds	155,500 –	181,500 –
3	Schedule C—Mortgages, Notes, and Cash	285,120 –	285,120 –
4	Schedule D—Insurance on the Decedent's Life (attach Form(s) 712)	200,000 –	200,000 –
5	Schedule E—Jointly Owned Property (attach Form(s) 712 for life insurance)	-0-	-0-
6	Schedule F—Other Miscellaneous Property (attach Form(s) 712 for life insurance)	712,200 –	775,200 –
7	Schedule G—Transfers During Decedent's Life (attach Form(s) 712 for life insurance)	-0-	-0-
8	Schedule H—Powers of Appointment	-0-	-0-
9	Schedule I—Annuities	-0-	-0-
10	Total gross estate (add items 1 through 9). Enter here and on line 1 of the Tax Computation	2,417,820 –	2,511,820 –

Item number	Deductions	Amount
11	Schedule J—Funeral Expenses and Expenses Incurred in Administering Property Subject to Claims	60,808 –
12	Schedule K—Debts of the Decedent	3,268 –
13	Schedule K—Mortgages and Liens	-0-
14	Total of items 11 through 13	64,076 –
15	Allowable amount of deductions from item 14 (see the instructions for item 15 of the Recapitulation)	64,076 –
16	Schedule L—Net Losses During Administration	-0-
17	Schedule L—Expenses Incurred in Administering Property Not Subject to Claims	-0-
18	Schedule M—Bequests, etc., to Surviving Spouse	-0-
19	Schedule O—Charitable, Public, and Similar Gifts and Bequests	7,500 –
20	Total of items 15 through 19—If you did not complete Schedule N, skip lines 21-24 and enter the line 20 amount on line 25	71,576 –
21	Intermediate taxable estate (subtract item 20 from item 10)	-0-
22	Maximum ESOP deduction (from Table D in the Instructions)	-0-
23	Enter the amount from Schedule N, line 8	-0-
24	Allowable ESOP deduction—enter the lesser of item 22 or 23	-0-
25	Total allowable deductions (add items 20 and 24). Enter here and on line 2 of the Tax Computation	71,576 –

Estate of: Karen L. Light

SCHEDULE A—Real Estate

(For jointly owned property that must be disclosed on Schedule E, see the Instructions for Schedule E.)

(Real estate that is part of a sole proprietorship should be shown on Schedule F. Real estate that is included in the gross estate under section 2035, 2036, 2037, or 2038 should be shown on Schedule G. Real estate that is included in the gross estate under section 2041 should be shown on Schedule H.)

(If you elect section 2032A valuation, you must complete Schedule A and Schedule A-1.)

Item number	Description	Alternate valuation date	Alternate value	Value at date of death
1	Brandy Run Farm, Botetourt County, VA Parcels 101-4711, 101-4712, 101-4713, 102-1008 (Appraisal attached)	12/17/88	$ 600,000.00	$ 600,000.00*
2.	Farmland, Botetourt County, VA Parcels 104-1178, 104-1179, 104-1180 (Appraisal attached)	12/17/88	$ 375,000.00	$ 375,000.00*
3.	Commercial Building, 187 River Road, City of Salem, VA Lot 7 Block 131-135 (Appraisal attached)	12/17/88	$ 90,000.00 (Sale Price)	$ 95,000.00 (Appraisal)
	* REFER TO SCHEDULE A-1			
	Total from continuation schedule(s) (or additional sheet(s)) attached to this schedule		-0-	-0-
	TOTAL. (Also enter on Part 5, Recapitulation, page 3, at item 1.)		$1,065,000.00	$1,070,000.00

(If more space is needed, attach the continuation schedule from the end of this package or additional sheets of the same size.)

Schedule A—Page 4

Estate of: Karen L. Light

SCHEDULE A-1—Section 2032A Valuation

Part 1.—Type of Election:

☐ **Protective election (Regulations section 20.2032A-8(b)).**—Complete Part 2, line 1, and column A of lines 3 and 4. (See instructions.)

☒ **Regular election.**—Complete all of Part 2 (including line 11, if applicable) and Part 3. (See instructions.)

Part 2.—Notice of Election (Regulations section 20.2032A-8(a)(3))

Note: *All real property entered on lines 2 and 3 must also be entered on Schedules A, E, F, G, or H, as applicable.*

1 Qualified use—check one ▶ ☒ Farm used for farming, *or*

▶ ☐ Trade or business other than farming

2 Real property used in a qualified use, passing to qualified heirs, and to be specially valued on this Form 706.

A Schedule and item number from Form 706	B Full value (without section 2032A(b)(3)(B) adjustment)	C Adjusted value (with section 2032A(b)(3)(B) adjustment)	D Value based on qualified use (without section 2032A(b)(3)(B) adjustment)
Schedule A 1.	$ 980,000.00	$ 600,000.00	$ 600,000.00
Schedule A 2.	540,000.00	375,000.00	375,000.00
Totals	$1,520,000.00	$ 975,000.00	$ 975,000.00

Attach a legal description of all property listed on line 2.

Attach copies of appraisals showing the column B values for all property listed on line 2.

3 Real property used in a qualified use, passing to qualified heirs, but not specially valued on this Form 706.

A Schedule and item number from Form 706	B Full value (without section 2032A(b)(3)(B) adjustment)	C Adjusted value (with section 2032A(b)(3)(B) adjustment)	D Value based on qualified use (without section 2032A(b)(3)(B) adjustment)
NONE	-0-	-0-	-0-
Totals	-0-	-0-	-0-

If you checked "Regular election" you must attach copies of appraisals showing the column B values for all property listed on line 3.

(Continued on next page)

Schedule A-1—Page 6

4 Personal property used in a qualified use and passing to qualified heirs.

A Schedule and item number from Form 706	B Adjusted value (with section 2032A(b)(3)(B) adjustment)	A (continued) Schedule and item number from Form 706	B (continued) Adjusted value (with section 2032A(b)(3)(B) adjustment)
Schedule F, 1 Farm Equipment	$ 225,000.00	"Subtotal" from Col. B, below left	$ 225,000.00
Subtotal	$ 225,000.00	**Total Adjusted Value**	$ 225,000.00

5 Enter the value of the total gross estate as adjusted under section 2032A(b)(3)(A). ▶ _____

6 Attach a description of the method used to determine the special value based on qualified use.

7 Did the decedent and/or a member of his or her family own all property listed on line 2 for at least 5 years of the 8 years immediately preceding the date of the decedent's death? . . . . ☒ **Yes** ☐ **No**

8 Were there any periods during the 8-year period preceding the date of the decedent's death during which the decedent or a member of his or her family:

	Yes	No
a Did not own the property listed on line 2 above?		X
b Did not use the property listed on line 2 above in a qualified use?		X
c Did not materially participate in the operation of the farm or other business within the meaning of section 2032A(e)(6)? . .		X

If "Yes" to any of the above, you must attach a statement listing the periods. If applicable, describe whether the exceptions of sections 2032A(b)(4) or (5) are met.

9 Attach affidavits describing the activities constituting material participation and the identity and relationship to the decedent of the material participants.

10 Persons holding interests. Enter the requested information for each party who received any interest in the specially valued property.

	Name	Address
A	Abraham L. Light	236 Mountain View Drive, Salem, VA 24153
B	Naomi K. White	2700 Grace Street, Richmond, VA 23225
C	Louise B. Hale	Rt. 2, Box 189, Charlottesville, VA 27901
D	Carroll A. Light, II	254 Mountain View Drive, Salem, VA 24153
E	Karen B. Cotswold	156 Shady Lane, London, OH 43140
F	Charles J. Hale	1807 Buckhead Drive, Atlanta, GA 30312
G	Dawn L. Hale	Rt. 2, Box 189, Charlottesville, VA 27901
H		

	Identifying number	Relationship to decedent	Fair market value	Special use value
A	429-06-1762	Son	$180,000	$125,000
B	538-14-0227	Daughter	$180,000	$125,000
C	601-23-4009	Daughter	$180,000	$125,000
D	611-40-6311	Grandson	$245,000	$150,000
E	612-59-0723	Granddaughter	$245,000	$150,000
F	613-21-6897	Grandson	$245,000	$150,000
G	615-86-0820	Granddaughter	$245,000	$150,000
H				

You must attach a computation of the GST tax savings attributable to direct skips for each person listed above who is a skip person. (See instructions.)

11 Woodlands election.—Check here ▶ ☐ if you wish to make a woodlands election as described in section 2032A(e)(13). Enter the Schedule and item numbers from Form 706 of the property for which you are making this election ▶ ....

You must attach a statement explaining why you are entitled to make this election. The IRS may issue regulations that require more information to substantiate this election. You will be notified by IRS if you must supply further information.

Schedule A-1—Page 7

Part 3.—Agreement to Special Valuation Under Section 2032A

Estate of:	Date of Death	Decedent's Social Security Number
Karen L. Light	6/17/88	070 :68 : 4921

We (list all qualified heirs and other persons having an interest in the property required to sign this agreement)

Abraham L. Light, Carroll A. Light, III, Naomi K. White, Karen B. Cotswold, Louise B. Hale, Charles J. Hale and Dawn L. Hale   ,

being all the qualified heirs and _____

_____ ,

being all other parties having interests in the property which is qualified real property and which is valued under section 2032A of the Internal Revenue Code, do hereby approve of the election made by _____ Abraham L. Light _____ ,

Executor/Administrator of the estate of _____ Karen L. Light _____ ,

pursuant to section 2032A to value said property on the basis of the qualified use to which the property is devoted and do hereby enter into this agreement pursuant to section 2032A(d).

The undersigned agree and consent to the application of subsection (c) of section 2032A of the Code with respect to all the property described on line 2 of Part 2 of Schedule A-1 of Form 706, attached to this agreement. More specifically, the undersigned heirs expressly agree and consent to personal liability under subsection (c) of 2032A for the additional estate and GST taxes imposed by that subsection with respect to their respective interests in the above-described property in the event of certain early dispositions of the property or early cessation of the qualified use of the property. It is understood that if a qualified heir disposes of any interest in qualified real property to any member of his or her family, such member may thereafter be treated as the qualified heir with respect to such interest upon filing a Form 706-A and a new agreement.

The undersigned interested parties who are not qualified heirs consent to the collection of any additional estate and GST taxes imposed under section 2032A(c) of the Code from the specially valued property.

If there is a disposition of any interest which passes or has passed to him or her or if there is a cessation of the qualified use of any specially valued property which passes or passed to him or her, each of the undersigned heirs agrees to file a **Form 706-A**, United States Additional Estate Tax Return, and pay any additional estate and GST taxes due within 6 months of the disposition or cessation.

It is understood by all interested parties that this agreement is a condition precedent to the election of special use valuation under section 2032A of the Code and must be executed by every interested party even though that person may not have received the estate (or GST) tax benefits or be in possession of such property.

Each of the undersigned understands that by making this election, a lien will be created and recorded pursuant to section 6324B of the Code on the property referred to in this agreement for the adjusted tax differences with respect to the estate as defined in section 2032A(c)(2)(C).

As the interested parties, the undersigned designate the following individual as their agent for all dealings with the Internal Revenue Service concerning the continued qualification of the specially valued property under section 2032A of the Code and on all issues regarding the special lien under section 6324B. The agent is authorized to act for the parties with respect to all dealings with the Service on matters affecting the qualified real property described earlier. This authority includes the following:

- To receive confidential information on all matters relating to continued qualification under section 2032A of the specially valued real property and on all matters relating to the special lien arising under section 6324B.
- To furnish the Service with any requested information concerning the property.
- To notify the Service of any disposition or cessation of qualified use of any part of the property.
- To receive, but not to endorse and collect, checks in payment of any refund of Internal Revenue taxes, penalties, or interest.
- To execute waivers (including offers of waivers) of restrictions on assessment or collection of deficiencies in tax and waivers of notice of disallowance of a claim for credit or refund.
- To execute closing agreements under section 7121.
- Other acts (specify) ▶ _____

By signing this agreement, the agent agrees to provide the Service with any requested information concerning this property and to notify the Service of any disposition or cessation of the qualified use of any part of this property.

		236 Mountain View Drive
Abraham L. Light	*Abraham L. Light*	Salem, VA 24153
Name of Agent	Signature	Address

The property to which this agreement relates is listed in Form 706, United States Estate (and Generation-Skipping Transfer) Tax Return, and in the Notice of Election, along with its fair market value according to section 2031 of the Code and its special use value according to section 2032A. The name, address, social security number, and interest (including the value) of each of the undersigned in this property are as set forth in the attached Notice of Election. 236 Mountain View Drive

IN WITNESS WHEREOF, the undersigned have hereunto set their hands at Salem, VA 24153   ,

this 3rd day of March, 1989

Qualified Heirs _____ ,

Signatures (attached additional signature sheet)

Other Interested Parties _____

Estate of: Karen L. Light

SCHEDULE B—Stocks and Bonds

(For jointly owned property that must be disclosed on Schedule E, see the Instructions for Schedule E.)

Item number	Description including face amount of bonds or number of shares and par value where needed for identification. Give CUSIP number if available.	Unit value	Alternate valuation date	Alternate value	Value at date of death
1	3500 Shares AT&T common stock (CUSIP NO: 123456789)	$35.50	12/17/88	$124,250.00	$143,500.00
2	400 Shares Pacific Gas & Light common stock (CUSIP NO: 987654321)	$23.25	12/17/88	$ 9,300.00	$ 12,000.00
3	200 Shares IBM common stock (CUSIP NO: 847532107)	$110.00	12/17/88	$ 22,000.00	$ 26,000.00
	Total from continuation schedule(s) (or additional sheet(s)) attached to this schedule . . .			-0-	-0-
	TOTAL. (Also enter on Part 5, Recapitulation, page 3, at item 2.)			$155,550.00	$181,500.00

(If more space is needed, attach the continuation schedule from the end of this package or additional sheets of the same size.)

(The instructions to Schedule B are in the separate instructions.)

Estate of: Karen L. Light

SCHEDULE C—Mortgages, Notes, and Cash
(For jointly owned property that must be disclosed on Schedule E, see the Instructions for Schedule E.)

Item number	Description	Alternate valuation date	Alternate value	Value at date of death
1	Checking Account #0180487695 Bank of Fincastle 1 Roanoke Street, Fincastle, VA 24090	12/17/88	$ 14,582.00	$ 14,582.00
2	Saving Account #246-58917 Bank of Fincastle 1 Roanoke Street, Fincastle, VA 24090	12/17/88	$ 65,011.00	$ 65,011.00
3	Money Market Account #Q-1487162 The Lion Fund 108 Third Avenue, New York, NY 10158	12/17/88	$205,527.00	$205,527.00
	Total from continuation schedule(s) (or additional sheet(s)) attached to this schedule . . .		-0-	-0-
	TOTAL (Also enter on Part 5, Recapitulation, page 3, at item 3.)		$285,120.00	$285,120.00

(If more space is needed, attach the continuation schedule from the end of this package or additional sheets of the same size.)

Schedule C—Page 11

111

Estate of: Karen L. Light

SCHEDULE D—Insurance on the Decedent's Life
You must attach a Form 712 for each policy.

Item number	Description	Alternate valuation date	Alternate value	Value at date of death
1	Automatic Flight Insurance AMEX Life Assurance Company 7372-889452-17003	12/17/88	$200,000.00	$200,000.00
2	Whole Life Insurance James Hancock Life Insurance Company K-108745-B-68104	12/17/88	($101,867.15)	($101,867.15)
	*NOTE: This policy not part of Gross Estate as decedent had no incidents of ownership			
	Total from continuation schedule(s) (or additional sheet(s)) attached to this schedule . . .		-0-	-0-
	TOTAL. (Also enter on Part 5, Recapitulation, page 3, at item 4.)		$200,000.00	$200,000.00

(If more space is needed, attach the continuation schedule from the end of this package or additional sheets of the same size.)

Schedule D—Page 13

112

Life Insurance Statement

OMB No. 1545-0022

Expires 2-28-91

Part I   Decedent—Insured (To Be Filed With United States Estate Tax Return, Form 706)

1 Decedent's first name and middle initial	2 Decedent's last name	3 Decedent's social security number (if known)	4 Date of death
Karen L.	Light	070-68-4921	6/17/88

5 Name and address of insurance company

James Hancock Life Insurance Company, 701 Lee Street, Philadelphia, PA 19103

6 Kind of policy	7 Policy number
Whole Life insurance	K-108745-B-68104

8 Owner's name. If decedent is not owner, please attach copy of application.	9 Date issued	10 Assignor's name. Please attach copy of assignment.	11 Date assigned
Naomi K. White	11/1/79	DNA	DNA

12 Value of the policy at the time of assignment	13 Amount of premium (see instructions)	14 Name of beneficiaries
DNA	$3,700.00 per annum	Jason A. Greene

15 Face amount of policy	$ 100,000.00
16 Indemnity benefits	$ -0-
17 Additional insurance	$ -0-
18 Other benefits	$ -0-
19 Principal of any indebtedness to the company deductible in determining net proceeds	$ -0-
20 Interest on indebtedness (item 19) accrued to date of death	$ -0-
21 Amount of accumulated dividends	$ -0-
22 Amount of post-mortem dividends	$ -0-
23 Amount of returned premium	$ 1,867.15
24 Amount of proceeds if payable in one sum	$101,867.15
25 Value of proceeds as of date of death (if not payable in one sum)	$ -0-

26 Policy provisions concerning deferred payments or installments.

Note: *If other than lump-sum settlement is authorized for a surviving spouse, please attach a copy of the insurance policy.*

----

27 Amount of installments	$ --

28 Date of birth, sex, and name of any person the duration of whose life may measure the number of payments.

----

29 Amount applied by the insurance company as a single premium representing the purchase of installment benefits	$ --

30 Basis (mortality table and rate of interest) used by insurer in valuing installment benefits.

----

31 Was the insured the annuitant or beneficiary of any annuity contract issued by the company? ☐ Yes ☒ No

32 Names of companies with which decedent carried other policies and amount of such policies if this information is disclosed by your records.

UNKNOWN

The undersigned officer of the above-named insurance company hereby certifies that this statement sets forth true and correct information.

Signature ▶ *Thomas A. Graves*   Title ▶ Vice President   Date of Certification ▶ 10/4/88

Instructions

Paperwork Reduction Act Notice.—We ask for this information to carry out the Internal Revenue laws of the United States. We need it to ensure that you are complying with these laws and to allow us to figure and collect the right amount of tax. You are required to give us this information.

The time needed to complete and file this form will vary depending on individual circumstances. The estimated average time is:

Form	Recordkeeping	Preparing the form
712	18 hrs., 25 min.	18 min.

If you have comments concerning the accuracy of this time estimate or suggestions for making this form more simple, we would be happy to hear

from you. You can write to IRS or the Office of Management and Budget at the addresses listed in the instructions of the tax return with which this form is filed.

Statement of Insurer.—This statement must be made, on behalf of the insurance company which issued the policy, by an officer of the company having access to the records of the company. For purposes of this statement, a facsimile signature may be used in lieu of a manual signature and if used, shall be binding as a manual signature.

Separate Statements.—A separate statement must be filed for each policy.

Line 13.—The premium to be reported on line 13 should be the annual premium, not the cumulative premium to date of death. If death occurred after the end of the premium period, the last annual premium should be reported.

Form **712** (Rev. 1-89)

Life Insurance Statement

OMB No. 1545-0022

Expires 2-28-91

Part I	Decedent—Insured (To Be Filed With United States Estate Tax Return, Form 706)

1 Decedent's first name and middle initial	2 Decedent's last name	3 Decedent's social security number (if known)	4 Date of death
Karen L.	Light	070-68-4921	6/17/88

5 Name and address of insurance company

James Hancock Life Insurance Company, 701 Lee Street, Philadelphia, PA 19103

6 Kind of policy	7 Policy number
Whole Life insurance	K-108745-B-68104

8 Owner's name. If decedent is not owner, please attach copy of application.	9 Date issued	10 Assignor's name. Please attach copy of assignment.	11 Date assigned
Naomi K. White	11/1/79	DNA	DNA

12 Value of the policy at the time of assignment	13 Amount of premium (see instructions)	14 Name of beneficiaries
DNA	$3,700.00 per annum	Jason A. Greene

15 Face amount of policy	$ 100,000.00
16 Indemnity benefits	$ -0-
17 Additional insurance	$ -0-
18 Other benefits	$ -0-
19 Principal of any indebtedness to the company deductible in determining net proceeds	$ -0-
20 Interest on indebtedness (item 19) accrued to date of death	$ -0-
21 Amount of accumulated dividends	$ -0-
22 Amount of post-mortem dividends	$ -0-
23 Amount of returned premium	$ 1,867.15
24 Amount of proceeds if payable in one sum	$101,867.15
25 Value of proceeds as of date of death (if not payable in one sum)	$ -0-

26 Policy provisions concerning deferred payments or installments.

Note: *If other than lump-sum settlement is authorized for a surviving spouse, please attach a copy of the insurance policy.*

....

....

27 Amount of installments	$ --

28 Date of birth, sex, and name of any person the duration of whose life may measure the number of payments.

....

....

29 Amount applied by the insurance company as a single premium representing the purchase of installment benefits	$ --

30 Basis (mortality table and rate of interest) used by insurer in valuing installment benefits.

31 Was the insured the annuitant or beneficiary of any annuity contract issued by the company? ☐ Yes ☒ No

32 Names of companies with which decedent carried other policies and amount of such policies if this information is disclosed by your records.

.............................UNKNOWN...

....

The undersigned officer of the above-named insurance company hereby certifies that this statement sets forth true and correct information.

Signature ▶ *Thomas A. Graves* Title ▶ Vice President Date of Certification ▶ 10/4/88

Instructions

Paperwork Reduction Act Notice.—We ask for this information to carry out the Internal Revenue laws of the United States. We need it to ensure that you are complying with these laws and to allow us to figure and collect the right amount of tax. You are required to give us this information.

The time needed to complete and file this form will vary depending on individual circumstances. The estimated average time is:

Form	Recordkeeping	Preparing the form
712	18 hrs., 25 min.	18 min.

If you have comments concerning the accuracy of this time estimate or suggestions for making this form more simple, we would be happy to hear from you. You can write to IRS or the Office of Management and Budget at the addresses listed in the instructions of the tax return with which this form is filed.

Statement of Insurer.—This statement must be made, on behalf of the insurance company which issued the policy, by an officer of the company having access to the records of the company. For purposes of this statement, a facsimile signature may be used in lieu of a manual signature and if used, shall be binding as a manual signature.

Separate Statements.—A separate statement must be filed for each policy.

Line 13.—The premium to be reported on line 13 should be the annual premium, not the cumulative premium to date of death. If death occurred after the end of the premium period, the last annual premium should be reported.

Form **712** (Rev. 1-89)

Estate of: Karen L. Light

SCHEDULE E—Jointly Owned Property
(If you elect section 2032A valuation, you must complete Schedule E and Schedule A-1.)

PART 1.— Qualified Joint Interests—Interests Held by the Decedent and His or Her Spouse as the Only Joint Tenants (Section 2040(b)(2))

Item number	Description For securities, give CUSIP number, if available.	Alternate valuation date	Alternate value	Value at date of death
	NONE			

	Total from continuation schedule(s) (or additional sheet(s)) attached to this schedule			
1a	Totals 1a		-0-	-0-
1b	Amounts included in gross estate (one-half of line 1a) 1b		-0-	-0-

PART 2.—All Other Joint Interests

2a State the name and address of each surviving co-tenant. If there are more than three surviving co-tenants, list the additional co-tenants on an attached sheet.

	Name	Address (number and street, city, state, and ZIP code)
A.		
B.		
C.		

Item number	Enter letter for co-tenant	Description (including alternate valuation date if any) For securities, give CUSIP number, if available.	Percentage includible	Includible alternate value	Includible value at date of death
		NONE			

	Total from continuation schedule(s) (or additional sheet(s)) attached to this schedule			
2b	Total other joint interests 2b		-0-	-0-
3	**Total includible joint interests** (add lines 1b and 2b). Also enter on Part 5, Recapitulation, page 3, at item 5		-0-	-0-

(If more space is needed, attach the continuation schedule from the end of this package or additional sheets of the same size.)

Schedule E—Page 15

Estate of: Karen L. Light

SCHEDULE F—Other Miscellaneous Property Not Reportable Under Any Other Schedule
(For jointly owned property that must be disclosed on Schedule E, see the Instructions for Schedule E.)
(If you elect section 2032A valuation, you must complete Schedule F and Schedule A-1.)

		Yes	No
1	Did the decedent at the time of death own any articles of artistic or collectible value in excess of $3,000 or any collections whose artistic or collectible value combined at date of death exceeded $10,000? . . . . If "Yes," full details must be submitted on this schedule.	X	
2	Has the decedent's estate, spouse, or any other person, received (or will receive) any bonus or award as a result of the decedent's employment or death? . . . . If "Yes," full details must be submitted on this schedule.		X
3	Did the decedent at the time of death have, or have access to, a safe deposit box? . . . . If "Yes," state location, and if held in joint names of decedent and another, state name and relationship of joint depositor.	X	

Abraham L. Light, Son
Salem Bank & Trust Company, 1 Main Street, Salem, VA 24153

If any of the contents of the safe deposit box are omitted from the schedules in this return, explain fully why omitted.

Does Not Apply

Item number	Description For securities, give CUSIP number, if available.	Alternate valuation date	Alternate value	Value at date of death
1	Farm Machinery for Brandy Run Farm (Refer Attached List)	12/17/88	$225,000.00	$235,000.00
2	Oil Painting "Mountain Morning" by C. F. Bransky	12/17/88	$ 7,200.00	$ 7,200.00
3	Royalties - Patent US-4891086 (Exp: 4-2011) Fiber-optic Switching Control Mechanism	12/17/88	$ 35,000.00	$ 35,000.00
4	100 Shares CAL, Ltd. private S Corporation Stock (closed 12-1-88)	12/17/88	$ -0-	$ 50,000.00
5	Set of Silver Serving Pieces	12/17/88	$ 31,500.00	$ 31,500.00
6	1984 Mercedes Benz 300 SD Sedan SN-1QR6785234B	12/17/88	$ 32,000.00	$ 35,000.00
7	300 Head Dairy Herd	12/17/88	$270,000.00	$270,000.00
8	Household Furnishings	12/17/88	$ 40,000.00	$ 40,000.00
9	Personal Items	12/17/88	$ 62,500.00	$ 62,500.00
10	Piano	12/17/88	$ 3,000.00	$ 3,000.00
11	Collection of First-Edition Books	12/17/88	$ 3,000.00	$ 3,000.00
12	1960 Ford Convertible SN - 06059581CJ	12/17/88	$ 3,000.00	$ 3,000.00
	NOTE: List and appraisals for above attached			
	Total from continuation schedule(s) (or additional sheet(s)) attached to this schedule . . .		-0-	-0-
	TOTAL. (Also enter on Part 5, Recapitulation, page 3, at item 6.)		$712,200.00	$775,200.00

(If more space is needed, attach the continuation schedule from the end of this package or additional sheets of the same size.)

Schedule F—Page 17

Estate of: Karen L. Light

SCHEDULE G—Transfers During Decedent's Life

(If you elect section 2032A valuation, you must complete Schedule G and Schedule A-1.)

Item number	Description For securities, give CUSIP number, if available.	Alternate valuation date	Alternate value	Value at date of death
A.	Gift tax paid by the decedent or the estate for all gifts made by the decedent or his or her spouse within 3 years before the decedent's death (section 2035(c))	X X X X X	-0-	-0-
B.	Transfers includible under section 2035(a), 2036, 2037, or 2038:			
1	NONE			
	Total from continuation schedule(s) (or additional sheet(s)) attached to this schedule		-0-	-0-
	TOTAL. (Also enter on Part 5, Recapitulation, page 3, at item 7.)		-0-	-0-

SCHEDULE H—Powers of Appointment

(If you elect section 2032A valuation, you must complete Schedule H and Schedule A-1.)

Item number	Description	Alternate valuation date	Alternate value	Value at date of death
1	NONE			
	Total from continuation schedule(s) (or additional sheet(s)) attached to this schedule . . .		-0-	-0-
	TOTAL. (Also enter on Part 5, Recapitulation, page 3, at item 8.)		-0-	-0-

(If more space is needed, attach the continuation schedule from the end of this package or additional sheets of the same size.)
(The instructions to Schedules G and H are in the separate instructions.)

Schedules G and H—Page 19

117

Estate of: Karen L. Light

SCHEDULE I—Annuities

Note: *Generally, no exclusion is allowed for the estates of decedents dying after December 31, 1984 (see instructions).*

		Yes	No
A Are you excluding from the decedent's gross estate the value of a lump-sum distribution described in section 2039(f)(2)? If "Yes," you must attach the information required by the instructions.			X

Item number	Description Show the entire value of the annuity before any exclusions.	Alternate valuation date	Includible alternate value	Includible value at date of death
1	Decedent was receiving a surviving spouse pension from the Quaker Assurance and Security Company which terminated at her death with no further value	12/17/88	-0-	-0-
	Total from continuation schedule(s) (or additional sheet(s)) attached to this schedule . . .		-0-	-0-
	TOTAL. (Also enter on Part 5, Recapitulation, page 3, at item 9.)		-0-	-0-

(If more space is needed, attach the continuation schedule from the end of this package or additional sheets of the same size.)

(The instructions to Schedule I are in the separate instructions.)

Schedule I—Page 2

Estate of: Karen L. Light

SCHEDULE J—Funeral Expenses and Expenses Incurred in Administering Property Subject to Claims

Note: *Do not list on this schedule expenses of administering property not subject to claims. For those expenses, see the Instructions for Schedule L.*

If executors' commissions, attorney fees, etc., are claimed and allowed as a deduction for estate tax purposes, they are not allowable as a deduction in computing the taxable income of the estate for Federal income tax purposes. They are allowable as an income tax deduction on Form 1041 if a waiver is filed to waive the deduction on Form 706 (see the Form 1041 instructions).

Item number	Description	Expense amount	Total Amount
1	**A. Funeral expenses:**		
	Oakey's Funeral Home - Transportation of Body from Utah	$ 565.00	
	Oakey's Funeral Home - Funeral Services, Casket	4,315.00	
	Oakey's Funeral Home - Granite Monument	2,145.00	
	Less Social Security Death Benefit	(255.00)	
	Total funeral expenses		$ 6,770.00
	B. Administration expenses:		
1	Executors' commissions—amount estimated/agreed upon/paid. (Strike out the words that do not apply.)		$35,000.00
2	Attorney fees—amount estimated/agreed upon/paid. (Strike out the words that do not apply.)		$ 6,000.00
3	Accountant fees—amount estimated/agreed upon/paid. (Strike out the words that do not apply.)		$ 2,100.00

		Expense amount	
4	Miscellaneous expenses:		
	Botetourt County Circuit Court - Letters Testamentary, Certified Copies, Fees	$ 96.00	
	Fincastle Herald - Legal Advertising	36.00	
	Roanoke Times & World News - Legal Advertising	108.00	
	Roanoke Land Appraisers, Inc. - Appraisals of real estate - 3	1,500.00	
	Jones & Smith Ltd. - Personal Property Appraisals	250.00	
	Fincastle Auction Company - Auction Fee	900.00	
	Additional Administration expenses - registered mail, copies, etc.	48.00	
	Agent's Commission - Sale of commercial building	8,000.00	
	Total miscellaneous expenses from continuation schedule(s) (or additional sheet(s)) attached to this schedule		$10,938.00
	Total miscellaneous expenses		
	TOTAL. (Also enter on Part 5, Recapitulation, page 3, at item 11.)		$60,808.00

(If more space is needed, attach the continuation schedule from the end of this package or additional sheets of the same size.) **Schedule J—Page 21**

Estate of: Karen L. Light

SCHEDULE K—Debts of the Decedent, and Mortgages and Liens

Item number	Debts of the Decedent—Creditor and nature of claim, and allowable death taxes	Amount unpaid to date	Amount in contest	Amount claimed as a deduction
1	Young Memorial Hospital - Provo, Utah - Final Bill (Net after Health Insurance settlement	-0-	-0-	$1,682.21
2.	APCO - Electric Service	-0-	-0-	104.32
3.	Highland Propane Co. - Gas	-0-	-0-	81.15
4.	C & P Telephone - Service	-0-	-0-	38.45
5.	American Express Co. - Airline Tickets	-0-	-0-	1,362.30

Total from continuation schedule(s) (or additional sheet(s)) attached to this schedule . . . .   -0-

TOTAL. (Also enter on Part 5, Recapitulation, page 3, at item 12.) $3,268.43

Item number	Mortgages and Liens—Description	Amount
1	NONE	

Total from continuation schedule(s) (or additional sheet(s)) attached to this schedule . . . .   -0-

TOTAL. (Also enter on Part 5, Recapitulation, page 3, at item 13.) . . . .   -0-

(If more space is needed, attach the continuation schedule from the end of this package or additional sheets of the same size.)

(The instructions to Schedule K are in the separate instructions.)

Schedule K —Page 23

Estate of: Karen L. Light

SCHEDULE L—Net Losses During Administration and Expenses Incurred in Administering Property Not Subject to Claims

Item number	Net losses during administration (Note: Do not deduct losses claimed on a Federal income tax return.)	Amount
1	NONE	
	Total from continuation schedule(s) (or additional sheet(s)) attached to this schedule	-0-
	TOTAL. (Also enter on Part 5, Recapitulation, page 3, at item 16.)	-0-

Item number	Expenses incurred in administering property not subject to claims (Indicate whether estimated, agreed upon, or paid.)	Amount
1	NONE	
	Total from continuation schedule(s) (or additional sheet(s)) attached to this schedule	-0-
	TOTAL. (Also enter on Part 5, Recapitulation, page 3, at item 17.)	-0-

(If more space is needed, attach the continuation schedule from the end of this package or additional sheets of the same size.)

(The instructions to Schedule L are in the separate instructions.)

Schedule L —Page 24

Estate of: Karen L. Light

SCHEDULE M—Bequests, etc., to Surviving Spouse

	Yes	No
1 Did any property pass to the surviving spouse as a result of a qualified disclaimer?		X

If "Yes," attach a copy of the written disclaimer required by section 2518(b).

2 **Terminable Interest (QTIP) Marital Deduction.**—Check here ▶ ☐ if you elect to claim a marital deduction for qualified terminable interest property (QTIP) under section 2056(b)(7). **You must complete Part 2 of Schedule M.**

Part 1.—Property Interests Which Are Not Subject to a QTIP Election

Item number	Description of property interests passing to surviving spouse	Value
1	NONE	
	Total from continuation schedule(s) (or additional sheet(s)) attached to this schedule	-0-
	Total value of property interests not subject to a QTIP election (enter here and on line 1 of Part 3 on the next page)	-0-

(If more space is needed, attach the continuation schedule from the end of this package or additional sheets of the same size.)
(The instructions to Schedule M are in the separate instructions.)   **Schedule M—Page 25**

Part 2.—Property Interests Which Are Subject to a QTIP Election

Item number	Description of property interests passing to surviving spouse (Describe portion of trust for which allocation is made.)	Value
1	NONE	

Total from continuation schedule(s) (or additional sheet(s)) attached to this schedule		-0-
A. Total value of property interests subject to a QTIP election	A	-0-

Part 3.—Reconciliation

1	Enter the total from part 1	1	-0-
2	Total interests passing to surviving spouse (add lines A and 1, above)	2	-0-
3a	Federal estate taxes (including section 4980A taxes) payable out of property interests listed on Parts 1 and 2	3a	-0-
b	Other death taxes payable out of property interests listed on Parts 1 and 2	3b	-0-
c	Federal and state GST taxes payable out of property interests listed on Parts 1 and 2	3c	-0-
d	Add items a, b, and c	3d	-0-
4	Net value of property interests listed on Schedule M (subtract 3d from 2). Also enter on Part 5, Recapitulation, page 3, at item 18	4	-0-

(If more space is needed, attach the continuation schedule from the end of this package or additional sheets of the same size.)

Schedule M—Page 26

Part 2.—Property Interests Which Are Subject to a QTIP Election

Item number	Description of property interests passing to surviving spouse (Describe portion of trust for which allocation is made.)	Value
1	NONE	
	Total from continuation schedule(s) (or additional sheet(s)) attached to this schedule	-0-
	A. Total value of property interests subject to a QTIP election . . . . **A**	-0-

Part 3.—Reconciliation

1	Enter the total from part 1	**1**	-0-
2	Total interests passing to surviving spouse (add lines A and 1, above)	**2**	-0-
3a	Federal estate taxes (including section 4980A taxes) payable out of property interests listed on Parts 1 and 2 **3a** -0-		
b	Other death taxes payable out of property interests listed on Parts 1 and 2 . . . . . . **3b** -0-		
c	Federal and state GST taxes payable out of property interests listed on Parts 1 and 2 . . . . . **3c** -0-		
d	Add items a, b, and c	**3d**	-0-
4	Net value of property interests listed on Schedule M (subtract 3d from 2). Also enter on Part 5, Recapitulation, page 3, at item 18	**4**	-0-

(If more space is needed, attach the continuation schedule from the end of this package or additional sheets of the same size.)

Schedule M—Page 26

Estate of: Karen L. Light

Note: *For qualified sales after October 22, 1986, and before February 27, 1987, see "Transitional Rules" in the instructions for Schedule N.*

SCHEDULE N —Qualified ESOP Sales (Under Section 2057)

1	Total qualified sales of employer securities to plans or cooperatives		**1**	-0-
2	Total 401(a) distributions (see instructions)	**2**		
3	Total transfers pursuant to options (see instructions)	**3**		
4	Net sales amount (see instructions)	**4**		
5	Total proceeds attributable to transferred assets (see instructions)	**5**		
6	Add lines 2 through 5		**6**	-0-
7	Subtract line 6 from line 1		**7**	-0-
8	Multiply line 7 by 50%. Enter the amount here and on Part 5, Recapitulation, page 3, at item 23		**8**	-0-

You must attach the required statement by the employer or cooperative officer. (See instructions.)

SCHEDULE O—Charitable, Public, and Similar Gifts and Bequests

		Yes	No
1a If the transfer was made by will, has any action been instituted to have interpreted or to contest the will or any provision thereof affecting the charitable deductions claimed in this schedule?			X
If "Yes," full details must be submitted with this schedule.			
b According to the information and belief of the person or persons filing the return, is any such action designed or contemplated? . . .			X
If "Yes," full details must be submitted with this schedule.			
2 Did any property pass to charity as the result of a qualified disclaimer?			X
If "Yes," attach a copy of the written disclaimer required by section 2518(b).			

Item number	Name and address of beneficiary	Character of institution	Amount
1	Hollins College - Hollins, Virginia 24020	Educational	$5,000.00
	American Red Cross -Roanoke Chapter 300 Church Avenue, Roanoke, VA 24011	Charitable	$2,500.00

Total from continuation schedule(s) (or additional sheet(s)) attached to this schedule.			-0-
3 Total		**3**	$7,500.00
4a Federal estate tax (including section 4980A taxes) payable out of property interests listed above . . .	**4a**	-0-	
b Other death taxes payable out of property interests listed above	**4b**	-0-	
c Federal and state GST taxes payable out of property interests listed above	**4c**	-0-	
d Add items a, b, and c		**4d**	-0-
5 Net value of property interests listed above (subtract 4d from 3). Also enter on Part 5, Recapitulation, page 3, at item 19 .		**5**	$7,500.00

(If more space is needed, attach the continuation schedule from the end of this package or additional sheets of the same size.)
(The instructions to Schedules N and O are in the separate instructions.)

How to Get IRS Forms and Publications

You can order federal tax forms and publications from the IRS Forms Distribution Center for your state at the address below. Use the order blank at the bottom of this page. Or, if you prefer, you can photocopy tax forms from reproducible copies kept at many participating public libraries. In addition, many of these libraries have reference sets of IRS publications which you can also read or copy—on the spot.

Alabama—Caller No. 848, Atlanta, GA 30370

Alaska—P.O. Box 12626, Fresno, CA 93778

Arizona—P.O. Box 12626, Fresno, CA 93778

Arkansas—P.O. Box 2924, Austin, TX 78769

California—P.O. Box 12626, Fresno, CA 93778

Colorado—P.O. Box 2924, Austin, TX 78769

Connecticut—P.O. Box 1040, Methuen, MA 01844

Delaware—P.O. Box 25866, Richmond, VA 23260

District of Columbia—P.O. Box 25866, Richmond, VA 23260

Florida—Caller No. 848, Atlanta, GA 30370

Georgia—Caller No. 848, Atlanta, GA 30370

Hawaii—P.O. Box 12626, Fresno, CA 93778

Idaho—P.O. Box 12626, Fresno, CA 93778

Illinois—P.O. Box 338, Kansas City, MO 64141

Indiana—P.O. Box 6900, Florence, KY 41042

Iowa—P.O. Box 338, Kansas City, MO 64141

Kansas—P.O. Box 2924, Austin, TX 78769

Kentucky—P.O. Box 6900, Florence, KY 41042

Louisiana—P.O. Box 2924, Austin, TX 78769

Maine—P.O. Box 1040, Methuen, MA 01844

Maryland—P.O. Box 25866, Richmond, VA 23260

Massachusetts—P.O. Box 1040, Methuen, MA 01844

Michigan—P.O. Box 6900, Florence, KY 41042

Minnesota—P.O. Box 338, Kansas City, MO 64141

Mississippi—Caller No. 848, Atlanta, GA 30370

Missouri—P.O. Box 338, Kansas City, MO 64141

Montana—P.O. Box 12626, Fresno, CA 93778

Nebraska—P.O. Box 338, Kansas City, MO 64141

Nevada—P.O. Box 12626, Fresno, CA 93778

New Hampshire—P.O. Box 1040, Methuen, MA 01844

New Jersey—P.O. Box 25866, Richmond, VA 23260

New Mexico—P.O. Box 2924, Austin, TX 78769

New York—

Western New York: P.O. Box 260, Buffalo, NY 14201

Eastern New York (including New York City): P.O. Box 1040, Methuen, MA 01844

North Carolina—Caller No. 848, Atlanta, GA 30370

North Dakota—P.O. Box 338, Kansas City, MO 64141

Ohio—P.O. Box 6900, Florence, KY 41042

Oklahoma—P.O. Box 2924, Austin, TX 78769

Oregon—P.O. Box 12626, Fresno, CA 93778

Pennsylvania—P.O. Box 25866, Richmond, VA 23260

Rhode Island—P.O. Box 1040, Methuen, MA 01844

South Carolina—Caller No. 848, Atlanta, GA 30370

South Dakota—P.O. Box 338, Kansas City, MO 64141

Tennessee—Caller No. 848, Atlanta, GA 30370

Texas—P.O. Box 2924, Austin, TX 78769

Utah—P.O. Box 12626, Fresno, CA 93778

Vermont—P.O. Box 1040, Methuen, MA 01844

Virginia—P.O. Box 25866, Richmond, VA 23260

Washington—P.O. Box 12626, Fresno, CA 93778

West Virginia—P.O. Box 6900, Florence, KY 41042

Wisconsin—P.O. Box 338, Kansas City, MO 64141

Wyoming—P.O. Box 2924, Austin, TX 78769

Foreign Addresses—Taxpayers with mailing addresses in foreign countries should send their requests for forms and publications to: IRS Distribution Center, P.O. Box 25866, Richmond, VA 23260.

Puerto Rico—Director's Representative, U.S. Internal Revenue Service, Federal Office Building, Chardon Street, Hato Rey, PR 00918

Virgin Islands—Department of Finance, Tax Division, Charlotte Amalie, St. Thomas, VI 00801

Detach At This Line

- -

Please follow these guidelines when ordering IRS forms and publications. This will help us process your order as quickly as possible. You will receive two copies of each form or schedule you request and one copy of each publication or instruction booklet. Please order only the items you need.

FORMS/INSTRUCTIONS/ SCHEDULES

PUBLICATIONS

- In the box to the left, list each form, instruction booklet, and schedule you need *by its number, not its title.* List forms and instructions in numerical order. List schedules in alphabetical order. (When ordering instructions or schedules, be sure to identify the forms they go with.)
- In the box to the right, list each publication you need *by its number, not its title.* Please list them in numerical order.
- Carefully print or type your name and address on the label provided below. This label will be used to send your order to you.
- Detach above and mail this order form and label to the IRS address shown for your area.

- -

Internal Revenue Service

Name

Number and street

City or town, State, and ZIP code

*U.S. G.P.O. 1988-506-945

CHAPTER 9

State Summary

Any citizen of the United States who is over the age of 19 and is of sound mind may write his or her own will. A will written entirely by hand by the Testator is known as a holographic will. In most cases, a holographic will does not need to be witnessed; however, it must be properly constructed and the handwriting verified (proven) as that of the Testator. At present, 30 states recognize holographic wills (2 of them only for persons in military service). A testamentary will is a will that is signed and dated before witnesses. The advantage of the testamentary will is that it can be much more readily "proven" as the will of the Testator. Consequently, if you now have a holographic will, we strongly recommend that you revoke it by a new testamentary will.

Summary of State Requirements

The requirements for writing a valid testamentary will are similar in all states and the District of Columbia. Differences in state requirements are summarized below.

WITNESSES. A testamentary will should be witnessed by "disinterested" persons, that is, people who are not mentioned in your will and who are not related to you. Louisiana and Vermont require three witnesses; the balance of the states require two witnesses to sign a will. If you own property in Vermont or Louisiana, it is advisable to have three witnesses. Your witnesses should also list their residential addresses next to their signatures.

SELF-PROVING. A self-proving certificate may be used to free witnesses from having to verify their signatures when the will is presented for probate. Self-proving is a convenience for your witnesses and can speed the probate process. Self-proving a will is optional but worth the brief additional time. All but five states (Mississippi, Vermont, Washington, West Virginia, and Wisconsin) recognize a properly notarized self-proving certificate.

COMMUNITY PROPERTY. There are nine community-property states: Arizona, California, Idaho, Louisiana, Nevada, New Mexico, Texas, Washington, and Wisconsin. In a community-property state, all property owned by a mar-

State Summary

State	Court Having Probate Jurisdiction	Holographic Wills Recognized	Number of Witnesses	Self-proving Recognized
Alabama	Probate Court)	Yes	2	Yes
Alaska	Superior Court	Yes	2	Yes
Arizona˙	Superior Court	Yes	2	Yes
Arkansas	Probate Court	Yes	2	Yes
California	Superior Court	Yes	2	Yes
Colorado	District Court (Denver: Probate Court)	Yes	2	Yes
Connecticut	Probate Court	No	2	Yes
Delaware	Court of Chancery	No	2	Yes
District of Columbia (DC)	Superior Court	No	2	Yes
Florida	Circuit Court	No	2	Yes
Georgia	Probate Court	No	2	Yes
Hawaii	Circuit Court	No	2	Yes
Idaho˙	District Court	Yes	2	Yes
Illinois	Circuit Court	No	2	No
Indiana	Circuit or Superior Court (Vigo and St. Joseph Counties: Probate Court)	No	2	Yes
Iowa	District Court	Yes	2	Yes

˙Community-property state.

ried couple is owned in one-half interest by each spouse. Exceptions include separate property brought into the marriage, property covered by valid prenuptial agreements, and property received through inheritance. Since community property does not include any right of survivorship, it is especially important to convey community-property interests with a valid will.

NONRESIDENT EXECUTOR. All states allow a nonresident to act as Executor, most with no restrictions. Some states allow only close family members or primary beneficiaries to act as a nonresident Executor. Additionally, some states require that a nonresident Executor have a state resident act as a personal agent and post a surety bond.

STATE TAXES. All states except Nevada impose federal credit estate taxes, and many impose one or more of the following: estate tax, gift tax, generation-skipping transfer tax and/or inheritance tax. Review the following State Summary for your state to identify applicable state taxes.

Living Will Recognized	Taxes				
	Federal Credit Estate	Estate	Gift	Generation-Skip Transfer	Inheritance
Yes	Yes	No	No	No	No
Yes	Yes	No	No	No	No
Yes	Yes	No	No	Yes	No
Yes	Yes	No	No	No	No
Yes	Yes	No	No	Yes	No
Yes	Yes	No	No	Yes	No
Yes	Yes	No	No	No	Yes
Yes	Yes	No	Yes	No	Yes
Yes	Yes	No	No	No	Yes
Yes	Yes	No	No	Yes	No
Yes	Yes	No	No	No	No
Yes	Yes	No	No	No	No
Yes	Yes	No	No	Yes	Yes
No	Yes	No	No	No	No
Yes	Yes	No	No	No	Yes
Yes	Yes	No	No	Yes	Yes

(*continued*)

State	Court Having Probate Jurisdiction	Holographic Wills Recognized	Number of Witnesses	Self-proving Recognized
Kansas	District Court	No	2	Yes
Kentucky	District Court	Yes	2	Yes
Louisiana*	District Court	Yes	3 3/5/7	Yes
Maine	Probate Court	Yes	2	Yes
Maryland	Orphan's Court (Hartford and Mongtomery Counties: Circuit Court)	Military (1 yr.)	2	Yes
Massachusetts	Probate and Family Court	No	2	Yes
Michigan	Probate Court	Yes	2	Yes
Minnesota	Probate Court	No	2	Yes
Mississippi	Chancery Court	Yes	2	Yes
Missouri	Circuit Court	No	2	Yes
Montana	District Court	Yes	2	Yes
Nebraska	County Court	Yes	2	Yes
Nevada*	District Court	Yes	2	Yes
New Hampshire	Probate Court	No	2	Yes
New Jersey	Surrogate's Court	Yes	2	Yes
New Mexico*	Probate or District Court	No	2	Yes
New York	Surrogate's Court	Military (War)	2	Yes
North Carolina	Superior Court	Yes	2	Yes
North Dakota	County Court	Yes	2	Yes
Ohio	Court of Common Pleas	No	2	Yes
Oklahoma	District Court	Yes	2	Yes
Oregon	Circuit or County Court	No	2	Yes
Pennsylvania	Common Pleas Court	Yes	2	Yes
Rhode Island	Probate Court	Yes	2	Yes
South Carolina	Probate Court	No	2	Yes
South Dakota	Circuit Court	Yes	2	Yes
Tennessee	Chancery Court (Davidson and Shelby Counties: Probate Court)	Yes	2	Yes

*Community-property state.

130

Living Will Recognized	Taxes				
	Federal Credit Estate	Estate	Gift	Generation-Skip Transfer	Inheritance
Yes	Yes	No	No	Yes	Yes
No	Yes	No	No	No	Yes
Yes	Yes	No	Yes	No	Yes
Yes	Yes	No	No	No	No
Yes	Yes	No	No	No	Yes
No	Yes	Yes	No	Yes	Yes
Yes	Yes	No	No	No	Yes
Yes	Yes	(x)	No	No	No
Yes	Yes	Yes	No	No	No
Yes	Yes	No	No	Yes	No
Yes	Yes	No	No	No	Yes
Yes	Yes	No	No	No	No
Yes	No	No	No	No	No
Yes	Yes	No	No	No	Yes
No	Yes	No	No	No	Yes
Yes	Yes	No	No	No	No
No	Yes	Yes	Yes	No	No
Yes	Yes	No	Yes	Yes	Yes
Yes	Yes	No	No	No	No
No	Yes	Yes	No	Yes	No
Yes	Yes	Yes	No	No	No
Yes	Yes	No	No	No	No
No	Yes	No	No	No	Yes
No	Yes	Yes	No	Yes	No
Yes	Yes	Yes	No	Yes	No
No	Yes	No	No	No	Yes
Yes	Yes	No	Yes	Yes	Yes

(continued)

State Summary (*continued*)

State	Court Having Probate Jurisdiction	Holographic Wills Recognized	Number of Witnesses	Self-proving Recognized
Texas·	County or Probate Court	Yes	2	Yes
Utah	District Court	Yes	2	Yes
Vermont	Probate Court	No	3	No
Virginia	Circuit Court	Yes	2	Yes
Washington·	Superior Court	No	2	Yes
West Virginia	County Commissioner	Yes	2	No
Wisconsin·	Circuit Court	No	2	No
Wyoming	District Court	No	2	Yes

·Community-property state.

Intestate Succession

All states have laws of succession governing the distribution of the estates of their residents who die without a valid will (intestate). The laws of intestate succession are necessarily rather complex, since they cover every possible combination of potential heirs that might survive the decedent. According to the American Bar Association, over 70 percent of Americans die without exercising their right to prepare a valid will. Whenever this is the case, the estate must be distributed in accord with laws of succession of the state of the decedent's domicile.

Although it is assumed that the readers of this book recognize the importance and value of having a current, valid will, it is also clear that other adult family members or friends may not have a similar understanding. They may feel that the state's distribution formula will be in accord with their wishes and that a will is therefore unnecessary. For example, it is a common misconception that if there are no children of the marriage, the surviving spouse will inherit the entire estate. Although this happens in 20 states, it does *not* in the other 30 and in the District of Columbia. If the decedent had children, distribution becomes even more complex, varying according to whether the children are offspring of the marriage and how many children there are. Further, if there were children who have died, then their intestate shares pass to their children (if any) *per stirpes*.

Unless all adult members of your family have a valid will, you may well need to petition the local probate court to be appointed as Administrator of a relative's estate at some time in the future. A brief summary of state intestate succession basics is presented on the following pages. This summary material may assist you in understanding the gross estate distribution and perhaps, more importantly, help you convince loved ones of their need for a valid will.

Living Will Recognized	Taxes				
	Federal Credit Estate	Estate	Gift	Generation-Skip Transfer	Inheritance
Yes	Yes	No	No	Yes	No
Yes	Yes	No	No	No	No
Yes	Yes	No	No	No	No
Yes	Yes	No	No	Yes	No
Yes	Yes	No	No	No	No
Yes	Yes	No	No	No	Yes
Yes	Yes	No	Yes	No	Yes
Yes	Yes	No	No	No	No

ELECTIVE SHARE

All states allow a surviving spouse to elect to receive a share of his or her spouse's estate rather than the bequests contained in the will. This elective, or "forced," share is an outgrowth of dower and curtesy rights and is intended to protect the surviving spouse against total disinheritance. The elective share is generally a portion of the probate estate although some states have expanded the assets covered to all property of the decedent, known as the "augmented estate." A petition for an elective share must be filed early in the probate process, usually within the first 60 days. The elective share is equal to, or, more frequently, less than, the spousal share under intestate succession. Often, no marital deduction can be taken for state estate and inheritance tax purposes, if an elective share is received. The elective share varies from state to state and recently has been subject to more frequent legislative changes. If you are considering petitioning an elective share, be sure to contact the local probate court to ascertain the actual amount that would be available at the time.

SPOUSAL SHARE

The state intestate succession summary tables that follow show the share that the surviving spouse would receive, which varies depending on the existence and number of other living potential heirs. These potential heirs are classified under five headings:

1. Children of the marriage *(per stirpes)*.
2. Other children of the deceased spouse *(per stirpes)*, which includes children from previous marriage(s) and illegitimate children.

3. No children but living parents of the deceased spouse.

4. No children and no living parents but brother(s) and/or sister(s) *(per stirpes)* of the deceased spouse.

5. No children, no living parents, and no brother(s) and/or sister(s).

In most states, in the last category (no children, no parents, and no brother(s) and/or sister(s) of the deceased spouse), the surviving spouse will inherit the entire estate. However, in Arkansas, Maine, Massachusetts, Oklahoma, Rhode Island, South Carolina, Texas, Vermont, and the District of Columbia, the surviving spouse will receive the entire estate only if there are also no living grandparents and no living descendants of the deceased spouse's grandparents as well.

Other special cases occur in Georgia, Mississippi, and Oklahoma, which provide for the spouse and children to receive equal shares, which means that the more children there are, the smaller the surviving spouse's share becomes. Arkansas requires the spouse to have been married for three years to obtain the full intestate succession share; otherwise, the share is diminished proportionally. Although not a community-property state, Oklahoma treats property gained during the marriage separately from other property. Louisiana, a community-property state, grants the surviving spouse a life estate interest in real property as long as the surviving spouse does not remarry, whereas Tennessee grants homestead and a one-year living allowance to the surviving spouse, not to be less than one-third of the estate. As you review this information, you will see how important having a valid will is to all your loved ones.

COMMUNITY-PROPERTY STATES

There are two types of property in community-property states: community property and separate property. Community property is all property owned by the couple during their marriage, and each has a one-half interest in it. Separate property is property owned solely by one spouse, such as an inheritance or assets identified in a valid prenuptial agreement. These two types of property are treated differently under intestate succession in all community-property states except Wisconsin.

LIFE ESTATE

A life estate is an interest in, and right to use, real property for the lifetime of the life estate holder. It is not ownership but rather a terminable interest. The following states and the District of Columbia grant life estate interests in real property to the surviving spouse under intestate succession. Louisiana (listed previously under community-property states) also grants spousal life estate interest if the surviving spouse does not remarry.

Surviving Spouse Share in Community-Property States

State	If Deceased Had Children		If Deceased Had No Children, and There Are		
	Children of Marriage Only	Other Children of Deceased	Living Parents of Deceased	No Living Parents but Living Siblings of Deceased	No Living Parents or Siblings of Deceased
	Then the Surviving Spouse Receives				
Arizona					
Community	½	None	All	All	All
Separate	All	½	All	All	All
California					
Community	All	All	All	All	All
Separate			½	½	All
1 Child	½	½			
2 or more	⅓	⅓			
Idaho					
Community	All	All	All	All	All
Separate	$50,000 + ½	½	$50,000 + ½	All	All
Louisiana					
Community	Life estate if no remarriage		All	All	All
Separate	None	None	None	None	All
Nevada					
Community	All	All	All	All	All
Separate			½	½	All
1 Child	½	½			
2 or more	⅓	⅓			
New Mexico					
Community	All	All	All	All	All
Separate	¼	¼	All	All	All
Texas					
Community	½	½	All	All	All
Separate	⅓	⅓	½	½	All*
Washington					
Community	All	All	All	All	All
Separate	½	⅓	¾	¾	All
Wisconsin					
Community	All	½	All	All	All
Separate	All	½	All	All	All

*If no living grandparents and no living descendants of deceased spouse's grandparents; otherwise, same as previous category.

Surviving Spouse Share in States with Life Estate Interests

State	If Deceased Had Children		If Deceased Had No Children, and There Are		
	Children of Marriage Only	Other Children of Deceased	Living Parents of Deceased	No Living Parents but Living Siblings of Deceased	No Living Parents or Siblings of Deceased
	Then the Surviving Spouse Receives				
Arkansas					
Real property	Life estate + ⅓	Life estate + ⅓	All*	All*	All*
Personal property	⅓	⅓	All*	All*	All*
Delaware					
Real property	Life estate	Life estate	Life estate	Life estate	All
Personal property	$5,000 + ½	½	$50,000 + ½	All	All
District of Columbia					
Real property	Life estate + ⅓	Life estate	Life estate + ⅓	Life estate + ⅓	All
Personal property	⅓	⅓	½	½	All**
Indiana					
Real property	Life estate	Life estate	¾	All	All
Personal property			¾	All	All
1 Child	½	½			
2 or more	⅓	⅓			
Kentucky					
Real property	Life estate + ⅓	Life estate + ⅓	½	½	All
Personal property	½	½	½	½	All
Rhode Island					
Real property	Life estate	Life estate	Life estate + $75,000	Life estate + $75,000	All**
Personal property	½	½	$50,000 + ½	$50,000 + ½	All**
West Virginia					
Real property	⅓	Life estate	All	All	All
Personal property	⅓	⅓	All	All	All

*If married 3 years; otherwise ½.
**If no living grandparents and no living descendants of deceased spouse's grandparents; otherwise, same as previous category.

Surviving Spouse Share in All Other States

State	If Deceased Had Children		If Deceased Had No Children, and There Are		
	Children of Marriage Only	Other Children of Deceased	Living Parents of Deceased	No Living Parents but Living Siblings of Deceased	No Living Parents or Siblings of Deceased
			Then the Surviving Spouse Receives		
Alabama	$50,000 + ½	½	$100,000 + ½	All	All
Alaska	$50,000 + ½	½	$5,000 + ½	All	All
Colorado	$25,000 + ½	½	All	All	All
Connecticut	$100,000 + ½	½	$100,000 + ¾	All	All
Florida	$20,000 + ½	½	All	All	All
Georgia	Equal shares with children (spouse ¼ minimum)		All	All	All
Hawaii	½	½	½	All	All
Illinois	½	½	All	All	All
Iowa	All	½ (Not less than $50,000)	All	All	All
Kanas	½	½	All	All	All
Maine	$50,000 + ½	½	$50,000 + ½	$50,000 + ½	All*
Maryland Minor child	$15,000 + ½ ½	$15,000 + ½ ½	$15,000 + ½	All	All
Massachusetts	½	½	$200,000 + ½	$200,000 + ½	All
Michigan	$60,000 + ½	½	$60,000 + ½	All	All
Minnesota	$70,000 + ½	½	All	All	All
Mississippi	Equal shares with children		All	All	All
Missouri	$20,000 + ½	½	$20,000 + ½	All	All
Montana			All	All	All
1 Child	All	½			
2 or more	All	⅓			

*If married 3 years; otherwise ½.
**If no living grandparents and no living descendants of deceased spouse's grandparents; otherwise, same as previous category.

(*continued*)

State	If Deceased Had Children		If Deceased Had No Children, and There Are		
	Children of Marriage Only	Other Children of Deceased	Living Parents of Deceased	No Living Parents but Living Siblings of Deceased	No Living Parents or Siblings of Deceased
	Then the Surviving Spouse Receives				
Nebraska	$50,000 + ½	½	$50,000 + ½	All	All
New Hampshire	$50,000 + ½	⅛	$50,000 + ½	All	All
New Jersey	$50,000 + ½	⅛	$50,000 + ½	All	All
New York			$25,000 + ½	All	All
1 Child	$4,000 + ½	$4,000 + ½			
2 or more	$4,000 + ⅓	$4,000 + ⅓			
North Carolina			$25,000 + ½	All	All
1 Child	$15,000 + ½	$15,000 + ½			
2 or more	$15,000 + ⅓	$15,000 + ⅓			
North Dakota	$50,000 + ½	½	$50,000 + ½	All	All
Ohio			All	All	All
1 Child	$30,000 + ½	$10,000 + ½			
2 or more	$10,000 + ⅓	$10,000 + ⅓			
Oklahoma			All	All	All
Marriage property	½	½			
Balance	½	Equal shares with children			
Oregon	½	½	All	All	All
Pennsylvania	$30,000 + ½	½	$30,000 + ½	All	All
South Dakota			½	½	All*
1 Child	½	½			
2 or more	⅓	⅓			
South Dakota			$100,000 + ½	$100,000 + ½	All
1 Child	½	½			
2 or more	⅓	⅓			
Tennessee	Homestead + 1 year living allowance (⅓ minimum)		All	All	All
Utah	$50,000 + ½	½	$100,000 + ½	All	All

*If no living grandparents and no living descendants of deceased spouse's grandparents; otherwise, same as previous category.

138

Surviving Spouse Share in All Other States (*continued*)

State	If Deceased Had Children		If Deceased Had No Children, and There Are		
	Children of Marriage Only	Other Children of Deceased	Living Parents of Deceased	No Living Parents but Living Siblings of Deceased	No Living Parents or Siblings of Deceased
	Then the Surviving Spouse Receives				
Vermont			$25,000 + ½	$25,000 + ½	All*
Real property					
1 Child	½	½			
2 or more	⅓	⅓			
Personal property	⅓	⅓			
Virginia	All	⅓	All	All	All
Wyoming	½	½	All	All	All

*If no living grandparents and no living descendants of deceased spouse's grandparents; otherwise, same as previous category.

Glossary

Abatement. Proportional reduction of general bequests when assets of estate are insufficient to meet such gifts fully.

Ademption. Situation occurring when an item of personal property given in a bequest is no longer a part of the final estate, rendering that bequest void.

Administrator A person or corporation appointed by the Court to manage the probate of the estate of a person dying without a valid will.

Annual exclusion. The amount that can be given by one person to another in a calendar year without incurring federal gift tax liability. Currently $10,000 per year.

Appraisal. A determination of the fair market value of property.

Attorney-in-fact. The role of a person you empower to act on your behalf through a power of attorney. This person does not have to be a lawyer.

Beneficiary. A person, organization, or institution named in a will to receive a portion of the estate. Also, someone who receives payment from an insurance policy or income from a trust.

Bequest. A gift of property made by a valid will.

Capacity. A legal adult who is of sound mind and not acting under menace, duress, or undue influence of others has the capacity (ability) to execute a valid will and other legal documents.

Codicil. An amendment to an original will that adds to, deletes from, or otherwise changes the provisions of the will; executed and witnessed in the same manner as the original will.

Common-law marriage. The cohabitation of a man and a woman appearing to be a legal marriage. In some states, this circumstance may have support and estate distribution implications.

Community property. A state-determined method of handling property acquired during marriage. Each spouse has a one-half interest in the subject property, regardless of the spousal financial contribution.

Contest. A challenge to the validity of a will, based either on procedural grounds or on questions as to the Testator's capacity.

Contingent beneficiary. A person who is designated to become a beneficiary if certain conditions set out in the will are fulfilled.

Curtesy. Widower's right to a share of his deceased wife's estate.

Dependent. A person who, by virtue of age or physical or mental condition, must rely on another for care and support.

Devise. A gift of real estate made by a will.

Domicile. Your permanent home, your legal residence; usually where you pay your taxes, vote, and receive correspondence.

Dower. Widow's right to a share of her deceased husband's estate.

Durable power of attorney. A power of attorney that designates an attorney-in-fact and that is still valid should you become incapacitated or incompetent.

Escheat. The taking of estate property by the state when there are no surviving beneficiaries or heirs to receive it.

Elective share. The right of a surviving spouse to choose to receive dower or curtesy rights; a share (usually ½) of the new probate estate rather than the amount in the will.

Estate. All assets, real and personal, and all liabilities left by a person who dies.

Estate tax. State and federal tax imposed on the transfer of property at death.

Execute. To complete and make valid a document by signing it.

Executor. A person named by the Testator in a will to administer the estate.

Fiduciary. A person who manages property and acts on behalf of another. Executors, Administrators, and trustees are fiduciaries.

Guardian. A person who has legal care and control over a minor child or an incompetent adult.

Heir. A person who may inherit property through an intestate succession.

Holographic will. A will written entirely by hand by the Testator.

Inheritance tax. A tax imposed by some states on the receipt of property from an estate. This tax is usually paid by, or on behalf of, the beneficiaries.

Intestate. Without a valid will.

Irrevocable. Cannot be changed, amended, revoked, or canceled.

Issue. Offspring or descendants, such as children and grandchildren.

Joint property. All property owned jointly with another party or parties.

Legacy. A gift of personal property made by a will.

Liabilities. All of a person's mortgages, debts, and obligations.

Life insurance trust. A trust funded by the proceeds from life insurance.

Liquid assets. Cash, and assets that can be readily converted into cash.

Living trust. A trust established during the trustee's life; also known as an *inter vivos* trust.

Living will. A signed, witnessed statement requesting that one's life not be prolonged by artificial means in cases of terminal illness or "permanent" unconsciousness.

Notary. A person authorized by state commission to certify, or attest to, documents, signatures, etc.

Per capita. Literally "By Head"; division in equal shares to surviving named beneficiaries.

Personal property. All property owned by a person except real property. Personal property can include personal effects, bank accounts, automobiles, boats, planes, stock, bonds, heirlooms, copyrights, patents, etc.

Personal representative. A state resident who receives legal notices on behalf of another, nonresident person.

Per stirpes. Literally, "By the root"; division of property in equal shares to the living descendants of a beneficiary who does not survive the Testator.

Power of attorney. A written authorization designating another person to act on your behalf (as your attorney-in-fact).

Prenuptial agreement. An agreement, executed prior to marriage clarifying individual ownership of assets.

Probate. The process of proving the validity of a will in the appropriate court.

Real property. All real estate (land, improvements, buildings) including residences, burial plots, commercial property, condominiums, and time-share units.

Residue. The remainder of an estate left after specific bequests have been made.

Revocable. Capable of being revoked, canceled, or changed.

Revoke. To cancel or terminate.

Right of survivorship. The right of a joint property owner to receive full ownership of jointly held property upon the death of the other joint owner. This right is generally set out in the deed or account agreement, and the property does not pass through the probate process.

Self-proving certificate. A notarized document stating that a will is properly witnessed.

Separate property. Anything that is not community property; often includes property owned before marriage and inheritances received.

Surety bond. A bond agreement that pledges to cover losses incurred as a result of willful, illegal administration.

Testament. A will, particularly one that deals with the disposition of personal property.

Testamentary trust. A trust established by a will.

Testator. A person who makes a valid will.

Title. Evidence of ownership.

Trust. An arrangement whereby a person transfers titled property (assets) to a trustee to hold and manage for the benefit of another person (the trust beneficiary).

Trustee. The person or organization that holds title and manages and distributes the trust property in accord with an existing trust agreement.

Will. A legal declaration of a person's wishes regarding the disposition of his or her estate after death, usually written and signed by the Testator and attested by witnesses.

Witness. A person who sees the maker actually sign a document and so certifies by signature on the document.

Index

Record Set

Using the Forms

ESTATE INVENTORY SHEETS

This section contains a set of estate and inventory sheets to assist you in organizing, preparing, and developing your estate plan. Listing the real and personal property of your estate can help you ensure that no assets are overlooked. The categories of property on the estate inventory sheets are transferable to U.S. Estate Tax Return (IRS 706) schedules as indicated in the following table.

Estate Inventory Sheets

Category	Transferable to IRS 706 Schedule	Page
Cash/Notes	C	R-3
Stocks/Bonds	B	R-4
Life insurance	D	R-5
Personal property	F	R-6
Annuities/Pensions	I	R-8
Real property	A	R-9
Joint real property	E	R-10
Farm/Business	A-1	R-11
Debts (2)	K	R-12
Estate summary (2)	—	R-14
Charitable gifts	O	R-16

A two-column format for listing asset values is used on the estate inventory sheets. The two columns can be used to list each spouse's property separately for estate planning purposes. An Executor can also use these estate inventory sheets with one column for date-of-death valuation and the other for alternate valuation (six months after date of death). If you are using the estate inventory sheets for estate planning, pencil entries are recommended, so that future updates can be made easily.

Generally, the assets listed on the first three inventory sheets will be the most liquid and, hence, the source of needed living expenses. When listing the value of personal property, recognize that original cost, replacement cost, market value, and auction value will differ. For property insurance purposes, replacement cost is usual. When valuing estate components, market value or auction value is more realistic. Values listed on the Farm/Business inventory sheet should be based on *use value,* if special valuation is anticipated; otherwise, use market value. Estate summary sheets are included so that the federal estate and state credit estate taxable estates can be calculated for planning purposes or settlement guidance.

EXECUTOR DATA SHEETS

Following the estate inventory sheets, there are two sets of Executor data sheets. These Executor data sheets provide space to list the key information your Executor will need. Information regarding organ donation; funeral arrangements; people to contact immediately; biographical background for obituary notices; location of keys, documents, and accounts; and beneficiaries and dependent/guardian concerns should be listed. These Executor data sheets are perforated so that you can detach them to give to your Executor for use when needed.

E S T A T E   I N V E N T O R Y

CASH/NOTES

Bank Accounts

Checking	Joint acct.?	Account #	Amount	Amount
First Security	yes	003-72060-59	$	$
			$	$
			$	$

Savings				
First Security	yes	003-80151-29	$	$
Id. Central Credit Union	yes	274654	$	$
			$	$

Certificates				
			$	$
			$	$
			$	$

IRAs

			Amount	Amount
			$	$
			$	$

Cash

			$	$

Safe Deposit Box

Location				
First Security Smile/overland		Box 306	$	$
			$	$

Notes Receivable

Maker _____ $_____ $_____

Address _____

Balance $_____ Security _____

Maker _____ $_____ $_____

Address _____

Balance $_____ Security _____

Total Cash/Notes $_____ $_____

R-3

ESTATE INVENTORY

STOCKS/BONDS

Stocks/Mutual Funds

Company	Number of shares	CUSIP number	Dollar value	Dollar value
_____	_____	_____	$_____	$_____
_____	_____	_____	$_____	$_____
_____	_____	_____	$_____	$_____
_____	_____	_____	$_____	$_____
_____	_____	_____	$_____	$_____
_____	_____	_____	$_____	$_____
_____	_____	_____	$_____	$_____
_____	_____	_____	$_____	$_____
_____	_____	_____	$_____	$_____
_____	_____	_____	$_____	$_____
_____	_____	_____	$_____	$_____
_____	_____	_____	$_____	$_____
_____	_____	_____	$_____	$_____

Bonds

Company/Government	Cost	Date	Dollar value	Dollar value
_____	$_____	_____	$_____	$_____
_____	$_____	_____	$_____	$_____
_____	$_____	_____	$_____	$_____
_____	$_____	_____	$_____	$_____
_____	$_____	_____	$_____	$_____
_____	$_____	_____	$_____	$_____
_____	$_____	_____	$_____	$_____
_____	$_____	_____	$_____	$_____
_____	$_____	_____	$_____	$_____
_____	$_____	_____	$_____	$_____
_____	$_____	_____	$_____	$_____

Total Stocks/Bonds $_____ $_____

——————————— **PERSONAL PROPERTY** (*continued*) ———————————

Jewelry

Description	Value	Value
_____	$_____	$_____
_____	$_____	$_____
_____	$_____	$_____
_____	$_____	$_____
_____	$_____	$_____
_____	$_____	$_____
_____	$_____	$_____

Tools/Hobby/Sporting Goods

Description	Value	Value
_____	$_____	$_____
_____	$_____	$_____
_____	$_____	$_____

Heirlooms and Collections

Description	Value	Value
_____	$_____	$_____
_____	$_____	$_____
_____	$_____	$_____

Antiques

Description	Value	Value
_____	$_____	$_____
_____	$_____	$_____
_____	$_____	$_____

Miscellaneous

Description	Value	Value
_____	$_____	$_____
_____	$_____	$_____
_____	$_____	$_____

Total Personal Property $_____ $_____

ANNUITIES/PENSIONS

Company_____   #_____

Agent_____   Amount $_____

Owner_____ Beneficiary_____

Company_____   #_____

Agent_____   Amount $_____

Owner_____ Beneficiary_____

Company_____   #_____

Agent_____   Amount $_____

Owner_____ Beneficiary_____

Company_____   #_____

Agent_____   Amount $_____

Owner_____ Beneficiary_____

Company_____   #_____

Agent_____   Amount $_____

Owner_____ Beneficiary_____

Company_____   #_____

Agent_____   Amount $_____

Owner_____ Beneficiary_____

Company_____   #_____

Agent_____   Amount $_____

Owner_____ Beneficiary_____

Company_____   #_____

Agent_____   Amount $_____

Owner_____ Beneficiary_____

Company_____   #_____

Agent_____   Amount $_____

Owner_____ Beneficiary_____

Total Annuities/Pensions $_____ $_____

E S T A T E   I N V E N T O R Y

————————————— **REAL PROPERTY** —————————————

Residence

House ☐   Condominium ☐   Co-op ☐   Other ☐

Description_____

_____

	Market value	Market value
Address_____	$_____	$_____

Deed in name of_____

Jointly owned ☐   Community property ☐   Co-owned ☐

Joint owner/Co-owner_____

Second/Vacation Home

Description_____

_____   Property #_____

	Market value	Market value
Address_____	$_____	$_____

Deed in name of_____

Jointly owned ☐   Community property ☐   Co-owned ☐

Joint owner/Co-owner_____

Commercial/Rental Property

Description_____

_____   Property #_____

	Market value	Market value
Address_____	$_____	$_____

Deed in name of_____

Jointly owned ☐   Co-owned ☐   Partnership ☐   Corporation ☐   Other ☐

Joint/Co-owner(s)_____

_____

Total Real Property	$_____	$_____

───────────────── **JOINT REAL PROPERTY** ─────────────────

Residence

House ☐   Condominium ☐   Co-op ☐   Other ☐

Description_____

_____

		Market value		Market value

Address_____

_____ $_____ $_____

Deed in name of_____

Jointly owned ☐   Community property ☐   Co-owned ☐

Joint owner/Co-owner_____

Second/Vacation Home

Description_____

_____   Property #_____

_____

Address_____   Market value   Market value

_____ $_____ $_____

Deed in name of_____

Jointly owned ☐   Community property ☐   Co-owned ☐

Joint owner/Co-owner_____

Commercial/Rental Property

Description_____

_____   Property #_____

_____

Address_____   Market value   Market value

_____ $_____ $_____

Deed in name of_____

Jointly owned ☐   Co-owned ☐   Partnership ☐   Corporation ☐   Other ☐

Joint/Co-owner(s)_____

_____

Total Joint Real Property $_____ $_____

—————————————————— FARM/BUSINESS ——————————————————

Farm

Real estate	$_____	$_____
Market value	$_____	$_____
Farm use value	$_____	$_____
Improvements	$_____	$_____
Equipment	$_____	$_____
Supplies	$_____	$_____
Livestock	$_____	$_____
Crops	$_____	$_____
Totals—Market value	$_____	$_____
Totals—Farm use value	$_____	$_____

Real estate % of Market value   _____%

Real estate % of Farm use value   _____%

Owners_____

_____

Operator(s)_____

Business

Real estate	$_____	$_____
Market value	$_____	$_____
Business use value	$_____	$_____
Improvements	$_____	$_____
Equipment	$_____	$_____
Supplies	$_____	$_____
Other	$_____	$_____
Totals—Market value	$_____	$_____
Totals—Business use value	$_____	$_____

Real estate % of Market value   _____%

Real estate % of Business use value   _____%

Owners_____

_____

Management_____

Buy–sell agreement   Yes___   No___

Business life insurance policy	$_____	$_____
	$_____	$_____
Total Business Life Insurance	$_____	$_____

R-11

ESTATE INVENTORY

———————— DEBTS ————————

Mortgages/Notes

Type_____ Original balance $_____

Security_____

Mortage/Note holder_____

Address_____

Location of document_____

Type_____ Original balance $_____

Security_____

Mortgage/Note holder_____

Address_____

Location of document_____

Type_____ Original balance $_____

Security_____

Mortgage/Note holder_____

Address_____

Location of document_____

Other Debts

Account	Number	Balance
_____	_____	$_____
_____	_____	$_____
_____	_____	$_____
_____	_____	$_____
_____	_____	$_____
_____	_____	$_____
_____	_____	$_____
_____	_____	$_____
_____	_____	$_____
_____	_____	$_____
_____	_____	$_____

Total Debts $_____

E S T A T E   I N V E N T O R Y

DEBTS

Mortgages/Notes

Type_____ Original balance $_____

Security_____

Mortage/Note holder_____

Address_____

Location of document_____

Type_____ Original balance $_____

Security_____

Mortgage/Note holder_____

Address_____

Location of document_____

Type_____ Original balance $_____

Security_____

Mortgage/Note holder_____

Address_____

Location of document_____

Other Debts

Account	Number	Balance
_____	_____	$_____
_____	_____	$_____
_____	_____	$_____
_____	_____	$_____
_____	_____	$_____
_____	_____	$_____
_____	_____	$_____
_____	_____	$_____
_____	_____	$_____
_____	_____	$_____
_____	_____	$_____
_____	_____	$_____

Total Debts $_____

───────────── **ESTATE SUMMARY** ─────────────

Estate Component Totals

Cash/Notes	$_____	$_____
Stocks/Bonds	$_____	$_____
Life Insurance	$_____	$_____
Personal Property	$_____	$_____
Annuities/Pensions	$_____	$_____
Real Property	$_____	$_____
Joint Real Property	$_____	$_____
Farm/Business	$_____	$_____
Inheritance _____	$_____	$_____
Gross estate totals	$_____	$_____
(less debts) _____	$ (_____)	$ (_____)
Balance	$_____	$_____
(less charitable gifts)	$ (_____)	$ (_____)
Balance	$_____	$_____
(less settlement cost estimate)	$ (_____)	$ (_____)
Actual estate before taxes	$_____	$_____
(less federal estate tax deduction)	$ (600,000)	$ (600,000)
Federal taxable estate	$_____	$_____

NOTE: If there is a federal taxable estate, an IRS 706 Return must be filed. A surviving spouse may use the amount of the marital deduction (Schedule M) to reduce the federal taxable estate to zero. Check with State Department of Taxation regarding other state estate, inheritance, gift and/or generation-skip tax liabilities.

Federal taxable estate (less state credit estate tax deduction)	$ (60,000)	$ (60,000)
State credit estate taxable estate	$_____	$_____

E S T A T E   I N V E N T O R Y

———————————— **ESTATE SUMMARY** ————————————

Estate Component Totals

Cash/Notes	$_____	$_____
Stocks/Bonds	$_____	$_____
Life Insurance	$_____	$_____
Personal Property	$_____	$_____
Annuities/Pensions	$_____	$_____
Real Property	$_____	$_____
Joint Real Property	$_____	$_____
Farm/Business	$_____	$_____
Inheritance	$_____	$_____
Gross estate totals	$_____	$_____
(less debts)	$ (_____)	$ (_____)
Balance	$_____	$_____
(less charitable gifts)	$ (_____)	$ (_____)
Balance	$_____	$_____
(less settlement cost estimate)	$ (_____)	$ (_____)
Actual estate before taxes	$_____	$_____
(less federal estate tax deduction)	$ (600,000)	$ (600,000)
Federal taxable estate	$_____	$_____

NOTE: If there is a federal taxable estate, an IRS 706 Return must be filed. A surviving spouse may use the amount of the marital deduction (Schedule M) to reduce the federal taxable estate to zero. Check with State Department of Taxation regarding other state estate, inheritance, gift and/or generation-skip tax liabilities.

Federal taxable estate (less state credit estate tax deduction)	$ (60,000)	$ (60,000)
State credit estate taxable estate	$_____	$_____

ESTATE INVENTORY

CHARITABLE GIFTS

Church

Full name	Address	Bequest(s)
_____	_____	_____
_____	_____	_____
_____	_____	_____
_____	_____	_____

Schools, Colleges

Full name	Address	Bequest(s)
_____	_____	_____
_____	_____	_____
_____	_____	_____
_____	_____	_____

Charities, Institutions

Full name	Address	Bequest(s)
_____	_____	_____
_____	_____	_____
_____	_____	_____
_____	_____	_____
_____	_____	_____

Other Nonprofit Organizations

Full name	Address	Bequest(s)
_____	_____	_____
_____	_____	_____
_____	_____	_____

Total Charitable Gifts $_____ $_____

Executor Data

Following are two detachable sets of executor data sheets. These sheets will enable you to organize and record information that will be of vital importance to your Executor. Each set has one sheet for each of these categories:

Immediate

Contacts

Personal

Final arrangements

Beneficiaries

Dependents/Guardians

Anne & Tim's Keys
in "drawer
Kase   1/7

E X E C U T O R   D A T A

──────────────── **IMMEDIATE** ────────────────

Location of Documents/Keys

Location of will_____

Date executed_____ # of Pages _____

Other documents_____

_____

_____

_____

Keys/Safety deposit box_____

_____

_____

_____

Burial/Funeral

Responsible person/Organization

Name_____

Address_____

Phone_____

Interment ☐   Cremation ☐   Crypt ☐   Other ☐

Service Type: Religious ☐   Fraternal ☐   Other ☐

Cemetery/Columbarium_____

_____

Body/Eye/Organ Donations

Organization/Group_____

Contact_____

Phone_____

Address_____

Donation_____

Organization/Group_____

Contact_____

Address_____

Phone_____

Donation_____

EXECUTOR DATA

CONTACTS

Accountant_____ Phone_____

Address_____

Attorney_____ Phone_____

Address_____

Banker_____ Phone_____

Address_____

Clergyman_____ Phone_____

Address_____

Doctor_____ Phone_____

Address_____

Executor_____ Phone_____

Address_____

Alternate Executor_____ Phone_____

Address_____

Insurance agent_____ Phone_____

Address_____

Insurance agent_____ Phone_____

Address_____

Trustee_____ Phone_____

Address_____

Relatives/Friends

Name_____ Phone_____

Address_____

Name_____ Phone_____

Address_____

Name_____ Phone_____

Address_____

Name_____ Phone_____

Address_____

————————————————— **PERSONAL** —————————————————

Full name_____ Birth date_____

Address_____

_____

Birthplace_____

Social security #_____ Medicare #_____

Military service #_____ Discharge date_____

Father's name_____ Birth date_____

Date deceased_____ Birthplace_____

Mother's maiden name_____ Birth date_____

Date deceased_____ Birthplace_____

Married ☐   Divorce ☐   Separated ☐   Widowed ☐   Single ☐   Remarried ☐

Spouse (name)_____ Marriage date_____

Social security #_____ Medicare #_____

Membership (Religious/Fraternal/Social, Other)_____

_____

_____

Children

Name_____ Birth date_____

Address_____

Name_____ Birth date_____

Address_____

Name_____ Birth date_____

Address_____

Name_____ Birth date_____

Address_____

Name_____ Birth date_____

Address_____

———————————————— **FINAL ARRANGEMENTS** ————————————————

Person responsible_____ Phone_____

Address_____

Alternate person_____ Phone_____

Funeral home (name)_____ Phone_____

Address_____

Location of service_____ Viewing: Yes ☐ No ☐

Address_____

Service type: Religious ☐ Military ☐ Fraternal ☐ Memorial ☐

Person officiating_____ Phone_____

Cemetery_____

Location_____

Section_____ Plot #_____

Interment_____ Entombment_____ Cremation_____

Location of deed_____

Music/Reading selections_____

_____

_____

_____

Flowers/Memorials_____

_____

Pallbearers   (Honorary)

_____   _____

_____   _____

_____   _____

_____   _____

_____   _____

EXECUTOR DATA

BENEFICIARIES

Name_____ Relationship_____
Address_____ Phone_____
Bequest(s)_____
_____

Name_____ Relationship_____
Address_____ Phone_____
Bequest(s)_____
_____

Name_____ Relationship_____
Address_____ Phone_____
Bequest(s)_____
_____

Name_____ Relationship_____
Address_____ Phone_____
Bequest(s)_____
_____

Name_____ Relationship_____
Address_____ Phone_____
Bequest(s)_____
_____

Name_____ Relationship_____
Address_____ Phone_____
Bequest(s)_____
_____

Name_____ Relationship_____
Address_____ Phone_____
Bequest(s)_____
_____

Name_____ Relationship_____
Address_____ Phone_____
Bequest(s)_____
_____

E X E C U T O R   D A T A

———— DEPENDENTS/GUARDIANS ————

Guardian(s)

Name——————————————————————— Relationship————————————————

Address———

Name——————————————————————— Relationship————————————————

Address———

Dependent Name

	Birth date	S.S. #
1. ———————————————	——————————	——————————
2. ———————————————	——————————	——————————
3. ———————————————	——————————	——————————
4. ———————————————	——————————	——————————

Medical Information

	Blood type	Doctor
1. ———————————————	——————————	——————————
2. ———————————————	——————————	——————————
3. ———————————————	——————————	——————————
4. ———————————————	——————————	——————————

Health Insurance (Company/Policy #) ————————————————————————

Special Instructions (Education, Religion, Guardianship agreement)

——

——

——

——

Assets (Accounts, Stocks, Bonds, Other) Manager: Guardian ☐   Executor ☐   Trustee ☐   Bank ☐   Other ☐

——

——

——

Insurance

Company/Agent——————————————————————— Amt./Type——————————

Policy #———————————— Address/Phone——————————————————————

Company/Agent——————————————————————— Amt./Type——————————

Policy #———————————— Address/Phone——————————————————————

Document Set

Using the Detachable Forms

There are a total of eight will forms in this section. They are perforated for easy removal and use. The completed forms, filled in in ink or on a typewriter, may be used as original documents. The forms may also be used as a guide if you prefer to type your own or need additional documents. Duplicate forms are provided so that you may revise or amend your estate plan when needed. Forms should be completed carefully with no crossed out words or erasures. All signatures should be written in ink. If you desire copies of your will and other documents, make them *before* you sign the originals. Never sign anything but the original document(s). *Do not* sign copies. Preparing a draft outline of your will can help avoid mistakes when you prepare the final document.

Be sure that your Executor, alternate Executor, guardian, and/or other persons involved with your estate plan are fully informed and consent to act on your behalf on mutually agreed-on terms. It is recommended that your chosen agents be given specific information as listed in the executor data sheets in the preceding record sets. Detailed information allows your Executor to act effectively and efficiently in settling your estate.

Forms Provided

Last will and testament (one-page form)—4 copies

Last will and testament (two-page form)—2 copies

Last will and testament (three-page form)—2 copies

Will self-proving certificate—4 copies

Codicil—2 copies

Codicil self-proving certificate—2 copies

Letter of instructions—2 copies

LAST WILL AND TESTAMENT

The three sets of will forms offer space to set out your plans, from a single bequest to extensive gifts or instructions. The first two sets of (one- and two-page) forms contain printed provisions that save expense to the estate. The following additional provisions are usually appropriate for all estates that name a beneficiary or other trusted person as Executor.

- The EXECUTOR named shall not be required to post surety bond.

- I direct that no outside appraisal be made of my estate unless required for estate tax purposes.

The last set of forms does not contain these provisions, although they may be written or typed on the forms, if desired. This last set has unnumbered pages, which may be used in sets or combined as needed. Be sure to indicate the page number and page total at the bottom of each page. You and your witnesses should also initial each page in the space provided at the bottom when you execute your will. All multiple-page wills should be fastened together before execution. Remember, you can't add pages after you've executed your will.

If you live in or have property in the states of Louisiana or Vermont, you must have three witnesses; everywhere else two witnesses are sufficient. Sign and date documents in front of all witnesses together at the same time and have them sign, date, and list their addresses on the document. You may keep the specific contents of wills and codicils confidential—your witnesses are attesting to your intent to make a will, not to the content of it. Remember, witnesses should *not* be relatives or others with an interest in your estate. Proper witness procedure should always be followed when executing your will or other documents.

WILL SELF-PROVING CERTIFICATE

Self-proving is an optional step that does not affect the validity of your will. A self-proving certificate, properly completed and notarized, eliminates the need for witnesses to be contacted when the will is presented for probate. The four self-proving certificates included may be completed by a notary public and attached to your will. To self-prove your will, you must appear before the notary with your witnesses and your original will. The notary can complete the self-proving certificate; after all have signed, the notary notarizes and seals the document before attaching it to your will. Be sure the expiration date of the notary commission is listed and that the notary seal is affixed. All states except Mississippi, Vermont, Washington, West Virginia, and Wisconsin recognize properly notarized self-proving certificates.

CODICIL

Two codicil forms are included for use if minor amendments to your will are needed. Have your original will before you when you prepare your codicil to verify its date of execution. Witness procedure for a codicil is the same as for a will.

CODICIL SELF-PROVING CERTIFICATE

A codicil may be self-proved in the same manner as a will in those states that recognize self-proving certificates. A self-proved codicil self-proves the will it amends. Note that the date of the original will must be filled in on the codicil self-proving certificate.

LETTER OF INSTRUCTION

Letters of instruction are provided to convey additional information to your executor, or appointed guardian, if required. You should date the letter of instruction and, if it contains specific directions regarding your estate, refer to the document by its date in your will. Remember, your will must set out the actual gifts of property or assets. Letters of instruction may contain messages or descriptions of heirlooms or property that are too lengthy or personal to be included in your will.

LAST WILL AND TESTAMENT

I, _____ , resident

of the _____ of _____ in the State of _____ ,

being of sound mind, do make and declare the following to be my LAST WILL AND TESTAMENT
and expressly revoke all my prior wills and codicils and certify that I am not acting under undue
influence, duress or menace.

I. EXECUTOR

I appoint _____ EXECUTOR
of this my LAST WILL AND TESTAMENT. If this EXECUTOR is unable to serve for any reason,

then I appoint _____ EXECUTOR.

The EXECUTOR is empowered to carry out all provisions of this WILL.

The EXECUTOR shall have all statutory powers available under State law.

The EXECUTOR named shall not be required to post surety bond. I direct that no outside appraisal
be made of my estate, unless required for estate tax purposes.

II. BEQUESTS

IN WITNESS WHEREOF, I have hereunto set my hand this _____ day of _____ , 19 _____ .

_____
(Testator signature)

III. WITNESSED

This LAST WILL AND TESTAMENT of _____
was signed and declared to be his/her LAST WILL AND TESTAMENT in our presence at his/her request and in his/her presence and the presence of each other as witnesses this _____

day of _____ , 19 _____ .

_____
(Witness signature)   (Address)

_____
(Witness signature)   (Address)

_____
(Witness signature)   (Address)

LAST WILL AND TESTAMENT

I, _____ , resident

of the _____ of _____ in the State of _____ ,

being of sound mind, do make and declare the following to be my LAST WILL AND TESTAMENT and expressly revoke all my prior wills and codicils and certify that I am not acting under undue influence, duress or menace.

I. EXECUTOR

I appoint _____ EXECUTOR
of this my LAST WILL AND TESTAMENT. If this EXECUTOR is unable to serve for any reason,

then I appoint _____ EXECUTOR.
The EXECUTOR is empowered to carry out all provisions of this WILL.
The EXECUTOR shall have all statutory powers available under State law.
The EXECUTOR named shall not be required to post surety bond. I direct that no outside appraisal be made of my estate, unless required for estate tax purposes.

II. BEQUESTS

IN WITNESS WHEREOF, I have hereunto set my hand this _____ day

of _____ , 19 _____ .

_____
(Testator signature)

III. WITNESSED

This LAST WILL AND TESTAMENT of _____.
was signed and declared to be his/her LAST WILL AND TESTAMENT in our presence at his/her request
and in his/her presence and the presence of each other as witnesses this _____

day of _____ , 19 _____ .

_____   _____
(Witness signature)   *(Address)*

_____   _____
(Witness signature)   *(Address)*

_____   _____
(Witness signature)   *(Address)*

LAST WILL AND TESTAMENT

I, _____ , resident

of the _____ of _____ in the State of _____ ,

being of sound mind, do make and declare the following to be my LAST WILL AND TESTAMENT and expressly revoke all my prior wills and codicils and certify that I am not acting under undue influence, duress or menace.

I. EXECUTOR

I appoint _____ EXECUTOR
of this my LAST WILL AND TESTAMENT. If this EXECUTOR is unable to serve for any reason,

then I appoint _____ EXECUTOR.
The EXECUTOR is empowered to carry out all provisions of this WILL.
The EXECUTOR shall have all statutory powers available under State law.
The EXECUTOR named shall not be required to post surety bond. I direct that no outside appraisal be made of my estate, unless required for estate tax purposes.

II. BEQUESTS

IN WITNESS WHEREOF, I have hereunto set my hand this_____ day
of _____ , 19 _____ .

_____
(Testator signature)

III. WITNESSED

This LAST WILL AND TESTAMENT of _____
was signed and declared to be his/her LAST WILL AND TESTAMENT in our presence at his/her request
and in his/her presence and the presence of each other as witnesses this _____

day of _____ , 19 _____ .

_____   _____
(Witness signature)   *(Address)*

_____   _____
(Witness signature)   *(Address)*

_____   _____
(Witness signature)   *(Address)*

LAST WILL AND TESTAMENT

I, _____ , resident

of the _____ of _____ in the State of _____ ,

being of sound mind, do make and declare the following to be my LAST WILL AND TESTAMENT
and expressly revoke all my prior wills and codicils and certify that I am not acting under undue
influence, duress or menace.

I. EXECUTOR

I appoint _____ EXECUTOR
of this my LAST WILL AND TESTAMENT. If this EXECUTOR is unable to serve for any reason,

then I appoint _____ EXECUTOR.
The EXECUTOR is empowered to carry out all provisions of this WILL.
The EXECUTOR shall have all statutory powers available under State law.
The EXECUTOR named shall not be required to post surety bond. I direct that no outside appraisal
be made of my estate, unless required for estate tax purposes.

II. BEQUESTS

IN WITNESS WHEREOF, I have hereunto set my hand this_____ day
of _____ , 19 _____ .

_____
(Testator signature)

III. WITNESSED

This LAST WILL AND TESTAMENT of _____
was signed and declared to be his/her LAST WILL AND TESTAMENT in our presence at his/her request
and in his/her presence and the presence of each other as witnesses this _____

day of _____ , 19 _____ .

_____ _____
(Witness signature)   *(Address)*

_____ _____
(Witness signature)   *(Address)*

_____ _____
(Witness signature)   *(Address)*

LAST WILL AND TESTAMENT

I, _____ , resident
of the _____ of _____ in the State of _____ ,
being of sound mind, do make and declare the following to be my LAST WILL AND TESTAMENT
and expressly revoke all my prior wills and codicils and certify that I am not acting under undue
influence, duress or menace.

I. EXECUTOR

I appoint _____ EXECUTOR
of this my LAST WILL AND TESTAMENT. If this EXECUTOR is unable to serve for any reason,

then I appoint _____ EXECUTOR.
The EXECUTOR is empowered to carry out all provisions of this WILL.
The EXECUTOR shall have all statutory powers available under State law.
The EXECUTOR named shall not be required to post surety bond. I direct that no outside appraisal
be made of my estate, unless required for estate tax purposes.

II. BEQUESTS

IN WITNESS WHEREOF, I have hereunto set my hand this_____ day
of _____ , 19 _____ .

_____
(Testator signature)

III. WITNESSED

This LAST WILL AND TESTAMENT of _____
was signed and declared to be his/her LAST WILL AND TESTAMENT in our presence at his/her request
and in his/her presence and the presence of each other as witnesses this _____

day of _____ , 19 _____ .

_____
(Witness signature)   *(Address)*

_____
(Witness signature)   *(Address)*

_____
(Witness signature)   *(Address)*

LAST WILL AND TESTAMENT

I, _____ , resident
of the _____ of _____ in the State of _____ ,
being of sound mind, do make and declare the following to be my LAST WILL AND TESTAMENT
and expressly revoke all my prior wills and codicils and certify that I am not acting under undue
influence, duress or menace.

I. EXECUTOR

I appoint _____ EXECUTOR
of this, my LAST WILL AND TESTAMENT. If this EXECUTOR is unable to serve for any reason,
then I appoint _____ EXECUTOR.
The EXECUTOR is empowered to carry out all provisions of this WILL.
The EXECUTOR shall have all statutory powers available under State law.

II. BEQUESTS

INITIALS _____ _____
             (Testator)   *(Witnesses)*
                          Page _____ of _____

INITIALS _____
(Testator)

_____
(Witnesses)

Page _____ of _____

IN WITNESS WHEREOF, I have hereunto set my hand this _____ day of _____ , 19 _____ .

_____
(Testator signature)

III. WITNESSED

This LAST WILL AND TESTAMENT of _____
was signed and declared to be his/her LAST WILL AND TESTAMENT in our presence at his/her request and in his/her presence and the presence of each other as witnesses this _____

day of _____ , 19 _____ .

_____   _____
(Witness signature)   (Address)

_____   _____
(Witness signature)   (Address)

_____   _____
(Witness signature)   (Address)

LAST WILL AND TESTAMENT

I, _____ , resident
of the _____ of _____ in the State of _____ ,
being of sound mind, do make and declare the following to be my LAST WILL AND TESTAMENT
and expressly revoke all my prior wills and codicils and certify that I am not acting under undue
influence, duress or menace.

I. EXECUTOR

I appoint _____ EXECUTOR
of this, my LAST WILL AND TESTAMENT. If this EXECUTOR is unable to serve for any reason,
then I appoint _____ EXECUTOR.
The EXECUTOR is empowered to carry out all provisions of this WILL.
The EXECUTOR shall have all statutory powers available under State law.

II. BEQUESTS

INITIALS _____ _____
              (Testator)   *(Witnesses)*
                              Page _____ of _____

IN WITNESS WHEREOF, I have hereunto set my hand this_____ day
of _____ , 19 _____ .

_____
(Testator signature)

III. WITNESSED

This LAST WILL AND TESTAMENT of _____
was signed and declared to be his/her LAST WILL AND TESTAMENT in our presence at his/her request
and in his/her presence and the presence of each other as witnesses this _____

day of _____ , 19 _____ .

_____
(Witness signature)   *(Address)*

_____
(Witness signature)   *(Address)*

_____
(Witness signature)   *(Address)*

WILL
SELF-PROVING CERTIFICATE

State of _____

County/City of _____

Before me, the undersigned authority, on this day personally appeared

_____
Testator
_____
Witness
_____
Witness
_____
Witness

known to me to be the Testator and Witnesses, respectively, whose names are signed to the attached or foregoing instrument and, all of these persons being by me first duly sworn, _____ _____ , the testator, declared to me and to the witnesses in my presence that said instrument is his/her LAST WILL AND TESTAMENT and that he/she had willingly signed or directed another to sign the same for him/her, and executed it in the presence of said witnesses as his/her free and voluntary act for the purposes therein expressed; that said witnesses stated before me that the foregoing will was executed and acknowledged by the testator as his/her LAST WILL AND TESTAMENT in the presence of said witnesses who, in his/her presence and at his/her request, and in the presence of each other, did subscribe their names thereto as attesting witnesses on the day of the date of said will, and that the testator, at the time of the execution of said will was over the age of eighteen years and of sound and disposing mind and memory.

_____   _____
(Testator signature)   *(Witness signature)*

                                         _____
                                         (Witness signature)

                                         _____
                                         (Witness signature)

Subscribed, sworn and acknowledged before me by _____ , the Testator,

and subscribed and sworn before me by_____

_____

_____ , Witnesses,

this _____ day of _____ , 19 _____ A.D.

Signed: _____
Notary Public
My Commission Expires: _____

(Seal)

WILL
SELF-PROVING CERTIFICATE

State of _____

County/City of _____

Before me, the undersigned authority, on this day personally appeared

_____
Testator

_____
Witness

_____
Witness

_____
Witness

known to me to be the Testator and Witnesses, respectively, whose names are signed to the attached or foregoing instrument and, all of these persons being by me first duly sworn, _____

_____ , the testator, declared to me and to the witnesses in my presence that said instrument is his/her LAST WILL AND TESTAMENT and that he/she had willingly signed or directed another to sign the same for him/her, and executed it in the presence of said witnesses as his/her free and voluntary act for the purposes therein expressed; that said witnesses stated before me that the foregoing will was executed and acknowledged by the testator as his/her LAST WILL AND TESTAMENT in the presence of said witnesses who, in his/her presence and at his/her request, and in the presence of each other, did subscribe their names thereto as attesting witnesses on the day of the date of said will, and that the testator, at the time of the execution of said will was over the age of eighteen years and of sound and disposing mind and memory.

_____
(Testator signature)

_____
(Witness signature)

_____
(Witness signature)

_____
(Witness signature)

Subscribed, sworn and acknowledged before me by

_____ , the Testator,

and subscribed and sworn before me by_____

_____

_____ , Witnesses,

this _____ day of _____ , 19 _____ A.D.

Signed: _____
Notary Public
My Commission Expires: _____

(Seal)

WILL
SELF-PROVING CERTIFICATE

State of _____

County/City of _____

Before me, the undersigned authority, on this day personally appeared

_____
Testator
_____
Witness
_____
Witness
_____
Witness

known to me to be the Testator and Witnesses, respectively, whose names are signed to the attached or foregoing instrument and, all of these persons being by me first duly sworn, _____

_____ , the testator, declared to me and to the witnesses in my presence that said instrument is his/her LAST WILL AND TESTAMENT and that he/she had willingly signed or directed another to sign the same for him/her, and executed it in the presence of said witnesses as his/her free and voluntary act for the purposes therein expressed; that said witnesses stated before me that the foregoing will was executed and acknowledged by the testator as his/her LAST WILL AND TESTAMENT in the presence of said witnesses who, in his/her presence and at his/her request, and in the presence of each other, did subscribe their names thereto as attesting witnesses on the day of the date of said will, and that the testator, at the time of the execution of said will was over the age of eighteen years and of sound and disposing mind and memory.

_____   _____
        (Testator signature)   *(Witness signature)*

                                            _____
                                                     (Witness signature)

                                            _____
                                                     (Witness signature)

Subscribed, sworn and acknowledged before me by

_____ , the Testator,

and subscribed and sworn before me by_____

_____

_____ , Witnesses,

this _____ day of _____ , 19 _____ A.D.

Signed: _____
                        Notary Public
My Commission Expires: _____

(Seal)

WILL
SELF-PROVING CERTIFICATE

State of _____

County/City of _____

Before me, the undersigned authority, on this day personally appeared

_____
Testator

_____
Witness

_____
Witness

_____
Witness

known to me to be the Testator and Witnesses, respectively, whose names are signed to the attached or foregoing instrument and, all of these persons being by me first duly sworn, _____

_____ , the testator, declared to me and to the witnesses in

my presence that said instrument is his/her LAST WILL AND TESTAMENT and that he/she had willingly signed or directed another to sign the same for him/her, and executed it in the presence of said witnesses as his/her free and voluntary act for the purposes therein expressed; that said witnesses stated before me that the foregoing will was executed and acknowledged by the testator as his/her LAST WILL AND TESTAMENT in the presence of said witnesses who, in his/her presence and at his/her request, and in the presence of each other, did subscribe their names thereto as attesting witnesses on the day of the date of said will, and that the testator, at the time of the execution of said will was over the age of eighteen years and of sound and disposing mind and memory.

_____
(Witness signature)

_____   _____
(Testator signature)   *(Witness signature)*

_____
(Witness signature)

Subscribed, sworn and acknowledged before me by

_____ , the Testator,

and subscribed and sworn before me by_____

_____

_____ , Witnesses,

this _____ day of _____ , 19 _____ A.D.

Signed: _____
Notary Public
My Commission Expires: _____

(Seal)

CODICIL

I, _____ , resident

of the _____ of _____ in the State of

_____ , being of sound mind, do make and declare this codicil to

be my LAST WILL AND TESTAMENT dated _____ , 19 _____ and

certify that I am not acting under undue influence, duress or menace.

In all other respects I ratify and confirm my Will and in witness whereof, I have hereunto set

my hand this _____ day of _____ , 19 _____ .

_____
(Testator signature)

This codicil to the LAST WILL AND TESTAMENT of _____

was signed and declared to be his/her codicil to his/her LAST WILL AND TESTAMENT in our presence

at his/her request and in his/her presence and the presence of each other as witnesses on this _____

_____ day of _____ , 19 _____ .

_____
(Witness signature)   (Address)

_____
(Witness signature)   (Address)

_____
(Witness signature)   (Address)

CODICIL

I, _____ , resident
of the _____ of _____ in the State of
_____ , being of sound mind, do make and declare this codicil to
be my LAST WILL AND TESTAMENT dated _____ , 19 ____ and
certify that I am not acting under undue influence, duress or menace.

In all other respects I ratify and confirm my Will and in witness whereof, I have hereunto set
my hand this _____ day of _____ , 19 ____ .

_____
(Testator signature)

This codicil to the LAST WILL AND TESTAMENT of _____
was signed and declared to be his/her codicil to his/her LAST WILL AND TESTAMENT in our presence
at his/her request and in his/her presence and the presence of each other as witnesses on this _____
_____ day of _____ , 19 ____ .

_____   _____
(Witness signature)   *(Address)*

_____   _____
(Witness signature)   *(Address)*

_____   _____
(Witness signature)   *(Address)*

CODICIL
SELF-PROVING CERTIFICATE

State of _____

County/City of _____

Before me, the undersigned authority, on this day personally appeared

_____
Testator

_____
Witness

_____
Witness

_____
Witness

known to me to be the Testator and Witnesses, respectively, whose names are signed to the attached or foregoing instrument and, all of these persons being by me first duly sworn, _____ _____ , the testator, declared to me and to the witnesses in my presence that said instrument is a codicil to his/her LAST WILL AND TESTAMENT dated _____ , 19 _____ , and that he/she had willingly signed or directed another to sign the codicil for him/her, and executed it in the presence of said witnesses as his/her free and voluntary act for the purposes therein expressed; that said witnesses stated before me that the foregoing codicil was executed and acknowledged by the testator as a codicil to his/her LAST WILL AND TESTAMENT in the presence of said witnesses who, in his/her presence and at his/her request, and in the presence of each other, did subscribe their names thereto as attesting witnesses on the day of the date of said codicil, and that the testator, at the time of the execution of said codicil was of sound and disposing mind and memory.

_____
(Witness signature)

_____   _____
(Testator signature)   *(Witness signature)*

_____
(Witness signature)

Subscribed, sworn and acknowledged before me by _____ , the Testator, and subscribed and sworn before me by_____ _____ _____ , Witnesses, this _____ day of _____ , 19 _____ A.D.

Signed: _____
                        Notary Public
My Commission Expires: _____

(Seal)

CODICIL
SELF-PROVING CERTIFICATE

State of _____

County/City of _____

Before me, the undersigned authority, on this day personally appeared

_____
Testator

_____
Witness

_____
Witness

_____
Witness

known to me to be the Testator and Witnesses, respectively, whose names are signed to the attached or foregoing instrument and, all of these persons being by me first duly sworn, _____

_____ , the testator, declared to me and to the witnesses in my presence that said instrument is a codicil to his/her LAST WILL AND TESTAMENT dated _____ , 19 ____ , and that he/she had willingly signed or directed another to sign the codicil for him/her, and executed it in the presence of said witnesses as his/her free and voluntary act for the purposes therein expressed; that said witnesses stated before me that the foregoing codicil was executed and acknowledged by the testator as a codicil to his/her LAST WILL AND TESTAMENT in the presence of said witnesses who, in his/her presence and at his/her request, and in the presence of each other, did subscribe their names thereto as attesting witnesses on the day of the date of said codicil, and that the testator, at the time of the execution of said codicil was of sound and disposing mind and memory.

_____
(Testator signature)

_____
(Witness signature)

_____
(Witness signature)

_____
(Witness signature)

Subscribed, sworn and acknowledged before me by

_____ , the Testator,

and subscribed and sworn before me by_____

_____

_____ , Witnesses,

this _____ day of _____ , 19 ____ A.D.

Signed: _____

Notary Public

My Commission Expires: _____

(Seal)

LETTER OF INSTRUCTIONS

LETTER OF INSTRUCTIONS